IN THE NAME OF HUMANITY

Speaking Out Against Circumcision

By
Joseph Lewis

THE BOOK TREE
San Diego, California

First published 1949
Eugenics Publishing Company
New York

New material, revisions and cover
© 2003
The Book Tree

ISBN 1-58509-229-0

Cover layout & design
Lee Berube

Printed on Acid-Free Paper
in the United States of America

FOREWARD

• How and why did circumcision begin?
• Does every male child that comes into the world have a birth defect?
• What outdated beliefs have also caused women to suffer for centuries?
• If we were created in the image of God, then why are we mutilating our children?

These questions and more are being asked by the author, Joseph Lewis. In this book he shares extensive research as to why he believes circumcision to be cruel, brutal and unnecessary, in addition to being completely unnatural. He also shares the true story of how he believes he saved the life of his grandson by insisting that the child not be circumcised.

Although this book shares a view that is not the accepted "norm", one may come away after reading it being far more educated on an alternative view of health that affects millions of people. Few books approach this subject so thoroughly and after reading it, questioning the practice of circumcision suddenly makes sense on a number of important levels.

It may be time for our society and doctors in general to rethink the trauma they inflict on defenseless babies, and for the reasons it is being done. Most people who have their children circumcised have done no research on the subject and simply concede to it because of tradition. But more and more people are beginning to investigate, and many who do so end up deciding against the procedure. Babies are not able to make a choice, so this book simply asks a responsible adult to do so—after first becoming informed.

This interesting and thought-provoking book is one of the few available today that provides an alternative and sometimes shocking view of the continued practice of circumcision.

Paul Tice

TO

ROBERT LEWIS EMORY

*Let Humanity Be Your
Guide in Life*

To free man from error is to give, not to take away.

—ARTHUR SCHOPENHAUER

Every great reform which has been effected has consisted, not in doing something new, but in undoing something old.

—HENRY THOMAS BUCKEL

To argue with a man who has renounced the use and authority of reason, and whose philosophy consists in holding humanity in contempt, is like administering medicine to the dead. . . .

—THOMAS PAINE

CONTENTS

INTRODUCTION

WHEN I was engaged in writing my book, *The Ten Commandments,* and proceeded to analyze the Fourth Commandment of the Decalogue, I read carefully the text of that Commandment, weighing each word as I read, not only for its expressed meaning, but also for any hidden or secret thought behind the word.

In reading the text of this Commandment, I was suddenly struck by the fact that the wife was not included among those particularly and specifically mentioned who should not "labor" on the Sabbath.

The next question was to discover why she was omitted. Why was only the wife excluded from the provisions of this Commandment? The failure to mention the wife specifically in this Commandment puzzled me for some time. What was the reason?

This, indeed, was a challenge.

The answer for this exclusion of the wife in the observance of this "sacred" day was to be found in the researches of anthropology. It was *because she was a woman!* And woman was taboo—a polluted being.

The origin of this taboo of women is based upon one of the most primitive superstitious beliefs. Savage man was unable to account for the mysterious apparatus of woman's peculiar physical make-up. The physical system of woman, with her monthly flow of "blood," often accompanied by excruciating pain, made primitive man, when compared to himself, look upon woman as having been "cursed" and, because of her "depraved" nature, responsible for bringing sin into the world.

The sight of blood brought consternation into the mind of primitive man. He was unable to account for its mysterious power. In one moment he saw a person flushed with life and strength; in another moment, he saw this same person inert, motionless, helpless and dead, only because the blood had oozed from his body. He was dead beyond all efforts to revive or resuscitate —of no more value than a clod of earth!

Primitive man was awed by the puzzling element of life that was in that blood. He began to fear it. Thus was born the superstitious belief that blood had power within itself to wreak vengeance or bring injury upon another.

For fear of being contaminated by the mysterious power inherent in blood, primitive man could conceive of no other way to avoid contamination than by making taboo those capable of polluting others; and, if contaminated, then some form of blood expiation was necessary for purification.

In the first category, woman was placed. Because of her sexual nature, woman became *taboo* as far as holy things were concerned, and the only way to avoid the direful consequences of having come in contact with her was by a blood sacrifice to free the victim from having been polluted.

The fear of contact with a woman, particularly during her period of menstruation, gripped with a paralyzing fear the mind of primitive man. The methods he devised to avoid such contact, and the schemes he invented to absolve himself after contact, are fantastic in the extreme.

Particularly among the ancient Hebrews did this superstition become an obsession.

Not only was woman, because of her sexual nature, *taboo* from holy and sacred things in the religious life of the Biblical Hebrew, but this primitive belief of blood contamination brought into existence elaborate and myriad forms of blood expiation, from that of uttering a prayer upon the killing of an animal to the cutting off of the foreskin of a male child on the *eighth* day of its birth.

As a direct result of this superstitious belief, circumcision came into existence among the early Hebrews *as a blood sacrifice.*

The ritual injunction, "And in the eighth day the flesh of his foreskin shall be circumcised," [1] following the birth of a male child, was in direct relation to the mother's state of taboo. *It was a blood sacrifice on behalf of the boy to cleanse himself of the contamination of having come in contact with the mother's "uncleanliness."*

The sole and primary purpose of this ritual performance was to obey the Biblical injunction that "Ye shall separate the Children of Israel from their uncleanness . . . unless . . . they defile my tabernacle. . . ." And as "a token of the covenant betwixt me and you. . . ." This blood sacrifice, based upon the primitive superstitious belief in blood contamination, was the sacred

[1] *Leviticus* 12, v. 1-4.

bond between the children of Israel and the Bible Deity, *and for no other reason.*

Health and hygiene were never even remotely associated with circumcision in Biblical times, and are merely an excuse for its continued practice today, because the primitive Hebrew knew nothing about health and hygiene in the modern sense of the word.

In fact, the Bible does not even contain the word hygiene!

The delusion of blood pollution in the Hebrew religion was carried over into Christianity and accounts for the New Testament edict that "without shedding of blood, is no remission of sin." [2]

The whole scheme of Christian salvation is based upon the belief that the crucifixion of Jesus was a blood atonement for the redemption of man for having been "shapen in iniquity, and in sin conceived." [3]

The Catholic Church, seeking to appropriate pagan celebrations as events of Christian tenet, designated the New Year as commemorating the submission of Jesus to the rite of circumcision in conformity with his having been born a Hebrew, and thereby fulfilling the "covenant of the law." That is why, in the calendar of the Catholic Church, the feast of the Saturnalia, the pagan celebration of the advent of the New Year, is now listed as the Feast of the Circumcision.

Since Jesus had fulfilled the covenant of the law "by submitting to this humiliation . . . which he was required to endure," according to Christian authority, [4]

[2] *Hebrews* 9, v. 22.
[3] *Psalm* 51, v. 5.
[4] *Catholic Encyclopedia,* Vol. 3, p. 779.

the Council of Jerusalem decided against the necessity of Christian children observing the rite of circumcision. And Saint Paul, in his *Epistle to the Galatians,* condemns the practice by Christians in these words: "Behold, I Paul say unto you, that if ye be circumcised, Christ shall profit you nothing." [5]

That is why Christian children were not obliged to be circumcised—because Jesus is supposed to have shed his blood as an expiation for man's having been born in "sin."

That this superstition also prevailed among other primitive tribes besides the Biblical Hebrews, and has been handed down from generation to generation in many and varied forms, is fully authenticated by authorities on anthropology.

That is probably why so great an authority as the late Sir James Frazer, after analyzing the prevalence of such customs among primitive and modern peoples, was forced to the conclusion that "in civilized society most educated people are not even aware of the extent to which savage ignorance survives at their doors."

I wonder if Shakespeare was thinking about this frightful and cruel mutilation upon an innocent and helpless infant when he said,

> "In religion,
> What damned error but some sober brow
> Will bless it, and approve it with a text
> . . ."

Nor is this ritual performance of blind superstition

[5] *Galatians* 5, v. 2.

without its tragic results. The number of deaths that result from circumcising a male child before he is physically able to stand such an ordeal might well be called the "slaughter of the innocents," yet some physicians today, who have come under the spell of this superstition, recommend circumcision as a "health and hygienic" measure. What a monstrous perversion of the truth!

In view of the prevalence of this superstitious practice and its growing adoption by otherwise intelligent people, I felt it somewhat of a duty to enlighten the public upon the primitive origin of circumcision and its meaningless, ritualistic performance.

By this means I hope to stop this devilish practice among civilized people and save countless millions of innocent and helpless children from this frightful and mutilating ordeal.

That is the reason for this book.

I sincerely hope, in the Name of Humanity, that it accomplishes its purpose.

IN THE NAME OF

HUMANITY

Chapter I

THE PRIMITIVE BELIEF
IN BLOOD POLLUTION

IN ORDER to understand fully the fear of blood and its polluting influence in the mind of the primitive Hebrew, and the major importance of some form of expiation to cleanse him from its contamination, it is necessary that we quote certain passages from the Bible. These indicate the intensity of the Hebrew's belief, and the necessity to protect himself from the peril which he believed would follow contact with this mysterious element so potent with evil consequences.

Without this evidence, it would be hard to believe, in view of our present knowledge, how primitive man could be so deluded and so frightened by the sight of blood.

With this evidence of the terrifying fear of blood and the necessity for a counter-reaction by some form of blood atonement, it is understandable why the Biblical Hebrew went to such horrifying lengths and committed such brutal, heartless and ridiculous acts to cleanse himself from blood contamination. It also explains why he made it so essential a part of his ritual observance, which, unfortunately, is responsible for the contagious spread of this superstition in our modern civilization.

So great was this fear that no Hebrew was permitted to eat the blood of an animal. It was not only taboo, but an expiatory rite was necessary to absolve one from such a guilt. This warning is first mentioned in *Genesis* 9, verse 4: [1]

> But flesh with the life thereof, *which is* the blood thereof, shall ye not eat.

This injunction is repeated in *Deuteronomy* 12, verse 23:

> Only be sure that thou eat not the blood: for the blood *is* the life; and thou mayest not eat the life with the flesh.

This prohibition against the eating of "the life with the flesh" is the reason why orthodox Jews even today will eat only "kosher" meat. To be "kosher," the animal or fowl must be killed and prepared for cooking in such a way that no blood remains in its body. All meat must be soaked in water for at least half an hour, salted and kept on a board for another half hour, so as to make certain that every drop of blood is extracted. Otherwise the prohibition, "Thou mayest not eat the life with the flesh" would be violated.

This accounts for the fact that porterhouse and tenderloin steaks and similar portions of the animal are not eaten by the orthodox. Before this meat could be

---

[1] The Biblical texts used in this book are taken from the King James version of the Bible, published by the American Bible Society.

eaten, all blood vessels would have to be removed to make it ritually edible.

A propitiative prayer is always said at the slaughter of animals or fowl to avoid the sin of shedding blood. There is some progress even in this custom because the ancient Israelites, in order to conform strictly to this ritual performance, had to bring the live animal or fowl to the temple. There it was slaughtered by the priest, who then performed a sacrificial ceremony by dashing the blood against the altar.

This superstitious custom is but another instance of the utter ignorance of the Biblical Hebrews concerning hygienic matters and the nutritive value of food.

Its detrimental effect is all too obvious.

In the strict interpretation of the belief in blood contamination, blood transfusions would be forbidden, with the inevitable result that hundreds of thousands of lives that are now saved would be sacrificed to this superstition.

In our day, the discovery of the composition of human blood has already been of incalculable benefit to mankind. Just think of the hundreds of thousands of soldiers in the last war alone who would have bled to death had it not been for Doctor Karl Landsteiner's discovery made in defiance of the "infallible" and "inspired" edicts of the Bible.

Much of the progress we have made in the field of science and human betterment can best be measured in direct ratio to our emancipation from our belief in the inerrancy of the Bible.

Even in the *Psalms* there is a prayer asking that we be spared the penalty of the guilt of blood.[2]

> Deliver me from bloodguiltiness, O God,
> thou God of my salvation: *and* my tongue
> shall sing aloud of thy righteousness.

"Bloodguiltiness" did not refer to killing, but to the contamination of blood without proper expiation. The use of the word "bloodguiltiness" reveals in itself the prevalence of the fear of blood pollution. Like all other superstitious peoples under the influence of *taboos,* the Hebrews were always provided with methods of atonement and expiation. They carried their superstitions to fanatical lengths, recording them in minute detail, and formulating their fears and taboos into a system of belief which became the dominant factor in their lives. This is plainly indicated in *Leviticus* 4, verses 1 to 3:

> And the Lord spake unto Moses, saying,
> 2 Speak unto the children of Israel, saying, If a soul shall sin through ignorance against any of the commandments of the Lord *concerning things* which ought not to be done, and shall do against any of them:
> 3 If the priest that is anointed do sin according to the sin of the people; then let him bring for his sin, which he hath sinned, a young bullock without blemish unto the Lord for a sin offering.

Let me emphatically state that there is no such thing as "sin." The idea of sin was born in the brain of primitive man who was unable to account for the injustices and inequalities that he faced in life and of the

[2] *Psalm* 51, v. 14.

hardships and suffering he was made to endure in his struggle to survive.

The primitive mind could conceive of no other explanation for the hardships of life except as "punishment for sin." This caused him to seek some solution to his difficulty, and so he devised means and methods to appeal to this wrathful Deity to be indulgent with him for the "sin" he had committed.

Since primitive man believed in sin and the necessity to be free of it, what could he do to appeal to this angry God who was forever tormenting him? By the strange process of superstitious reasoning, he believed that only by a blood sacrifice could sin be removed, and here is one of the methods recorded in *Leviticus* 4, verses 4 to 12:

> 4 And he shall bring the bullock unto the door of the tabernacle of the congregation before the Lord; and shall lay his hand upon the bullock's head, and kill the bullock before the Lord.
>
> 5 And the priest that is anointed shall take of the bullock's blood, and bring it to the tabernacle of the congregation:
>
> 6 And the priest shall dip his finger in the blood, and sprinkle of the blood seven times before the Lord, before the veil of the sanctuary.
>
> 7 And the priest shall put *some* of the blood upon the horns of the altar of sweet incense before the Lord, which *is* in the tabernacle of the congregation; and shall pour all the blood of the bullock at the bottom of the altar of the burnt offering, which *is at* the door of the tabernacle of the congregation.
>
> 8 And he shall take off from it all the fat of the bullock for the sin offering; the fat that covereth the inwards, and all the fat that *is* upon the inwards,

9 And the two kidneys, and the fat that *is* upon them, which *is* by the flanks, and the caul above the liver, with the kidneys, it shall he take away.

10 As it was taken off from the bullock of the sacrifice of peace offerings: and the priest shall burn them upon the altar of the burnt offering.

11 And the skin of the bullock, and all his flesh, with his head, and with his legs, and his inwards, and his dung,

12 Even the whole bullock shall he carry forth without the camp unto a clean place, where the ashes are poured out, and burn him on the wood with fire: where the ashes are poured out shall he be burnt.

What saving grace is inherent in such a sacrifice? It is the pitiful attempt by primitive man to rely upon some magic formula to minimize the hardships of life.

How could the spilling of the innocent blood of a "bullock without blemish" wipe out the commission of a sin? What potency did this formula possess when the priest "shall dip his finger in the blood, and sprinkle of the blood seven times before the Lord ...?" Why the further disposition of the animal, as the text describes?

The fear of blood pollution and the necessity for its expiation are also shown in I *Samuel* 14, verses 31 to 33:

31 And they smote the Philistines that day from Michmash to Aijalon: and the people were very faint.

32 And the people flew upon the spoil, and took sheep, and oxen, and calves, and slew *them* on the ground: and the people did eat *them* with the blood.

33 ¶ Then they told Saul, saying, Behold, the people sin against the Lord, in that they eat with the blood. And he said, Ye have transgressed: roll a great stone unto me this day.

Their transgression had to be expiated, and of what did this ceremony of purification consist? The "sinner" had to "roll a great stone unto me this day," in the belief that this useless exertion of one's strength would expiate the sin caused by the violation of the *taboo*.

Further evidence of the dominant fear among the ancient Hebrews [3] is found in *Numbers* 35, verses 33 and 34:

> 33 So ye shall not pollute the land wherein ye *are:* for blood it defileth the land: and the land cannot be cleansed of the blood that is shed therein, but by the blood of him that shed it.
> 34 Defile not therefore the land which ye shall inhabit, wherein I dwell: for I the Lord dwell among the children of Israel.

Proof of the belief in blood pollution is the extremely significant statement in the above verse that "the land cannot be cleansed of the blood that is shed therein, but by blood of him that shed it." This is the basis for the practice of blood atonement. The necessity for expiation is indicative of the fear that obsessed the Biblical Hebrew.

This same fear is expressed in *Genesis* 4, verses 8 to 13, and reveals how deeply ingrained was this superstition among the Children of Israel:

> 8 And Cain talked with Abel his brother: and it came to pass when they were in the field, that Cain rose up against Abel his brother, and slew him.

[3] For the prevalence of this superstition among other primitive tribes of the same cultural level as the Biblical Hebrews, see *The Ten Commandments,* by Joseph Lewis.

> 9 And the Lord said unto Cain, Where *is* Abel thy brother? And he said, I know not: *Am* I my brother's keeper?
>
> 10 And he said, What hast thou done? the voice of thy brother's blood crieth unto me from the ground.
>
> 11 And now *art* thou cursed from the earth, which hath opened her mouth to receive thy brother's blood from thy hand.
>
> 12 When thou tillest the ground, it shall not henceforth yield unto thee her strength; a fugitive and a vagabond shalt thou be in the earth.
>
> 13 And Cain said unto the Lord, My punishment *is* greater than I can bear.

". . . the voice of thy brother's *blood* crieth unto me from the ground." And this blood will pollute the earth and prevent it from yielding fruit. Verses 14 to 16, following, also state that Cain is to be haunted throughout his life by the spirit of the one whose blood has been shed.

> 14 Behold, thou hast driven me out this day from the face of the earth; and from thy face shall I be hid; and I shall be a fugitive and a vagabond in the earth; and it shall come to pass, *that* every one that findeth me shall slay me.
>
> 15 And the Lord said unto him, Therefore whosoever slayeth Cain, vengeance shall be taken on him sevenfold. And the Lord set a mark upon Cain, lest any finding him should kill him.
>
> 16 And Cain went out from the presence of the Lord, and dwelt in the land of Nod, on the east of Eden.

This taboo was carried over into Christianity when Jesus said, "This is my blood of the New Testament which is shed for many." [4] That is why heretics were burned at the stake—to avoid the spilling of blood.

[4] *Mark* 14, v. 24.

The Christian doctrine was that "the hands which had to distribute the blood of the Lamb were not to be polluted with the blood of those for whose salvation it was shed!"

This "token" of blood sacrifice which prevailed with such persistence among the Children of Israel not only signified a compact with their God but was also the means of cementing family ties and agreements among themselves.

The intermingling of blood as a method of sealing bargains and binding marriages was also prevalent; in fact, it gave to contracts an additional sacred safeguard. It was believed that by sealing these agreements with blood, it made God a witness to the deed.[5]

In propitiating the gods, the greater the sacrifice the more likely the forgiveness or the granting of the favors asked. The more valuable the offering, the more certain was the belief of appeasement, hence, the prevalence in primitive society of the sacrifice of the firstborn to a "jealous and wrathful god."

Next to the sacrifice of the life was the blood, which was the life, and, therefore a *token* of life was sacrificed instead of all of it. That is why circumcision among the Biblical Hebrews was a *token* of the covenant between the clan and its god.[6]

---

[5] For additional instances of the prevalence of this superstitious belief among primitive people, and its prevalence even today among some backward people, see Frazer, *Taboo and the Perils of the Soul;* Trumbull, *The Blood Covenant;* Mantegazza, *The Sexual Relations of Mankind;* Westermarck, *The Origin and Development of Moral Ideas.*

[6] Trumbull, *loc. cit.,* p. 300.

Its importance is emphasized by this injunction of
Moses to the Children of Israel: [7]

> 3 And Moses came and told the
> people all the words of the Lord, and
> all the judgments: and all the people
> answered with one voice, and said, All
> the words which the Lord hath said will
> we do.
>
> 4 And Moses wrote all the words of the
> Lord, and rose up early in the morning,
> and builded an altar under the hill, and
> twelve pillars, according to the twelve
> tribes of Israel.
>
> 5 And he sent young men of the chil-
> dren of Israel, which offered burnt
> offerings, and sacrificed peace offerings
> of oxen unto the Lord.
>
> 6 And Moses took half of the blood,
> and put *it* in basins; and half of the
> blood he sprinkled on the altar.
>
> 7 And he took the book of the cove-
> nant, and read in the audience of the
> people: and they said, All that the Lord
> hath said will we do, and be obe-
> dient.
>
> 8 And Moses took the blood, and
> sprinkled *it* on the people, and said, Be-
> hold the blood of the covenant, which
> the Lord hath made with you concern-
> ing all these words.

Another very significant custom which has an important bearing upon this belief in blood pollution was
the establishment of a sanctuary for those who killed
accidentally, that they might escape the revenge of the
victim and save the land from the curse of blood contamination. [8]

These cities of sanctuary were established so that
blood shed within the confines of the tribe might be
expiated, and thereby prevent the curse of blood pollution from falling upon the whole tribe.

[7] *Exodus* 24, vs. 3 to 8.
[8] *Deuteronomy* 19, vs. 1 to 9.

Even David was not permitted to build a house "of the Lord" nor become associated with any holy or sacred edifice because he had shed blood which had not been properly atoned for.

The following passage also reveals the taboo regarding the shedding of blood: [9]

> 2 Then David the king stood up upon his feet, and said, Hear me, my brethren, and my people: *As for me,* I *had* in mine heart to build a house of rest for the ark of the covenant of the Lord, and for the footstool of our God, and had made ready for the building:
> 3 But God said unto me, Thou shalt not build a house for my name, because thou *hast been* a man of war, and hast shed blood.

David could not build a temple to the Lord because he had shed blood and, according to Biblical tradition, the building of the temple was left to Solomon, his son.

The early Hebrew priests refrained from shedding blood, except for sacrificial purposes, and then only when accompanied by expiatory prayers.

It was inevitable that this superstition should develop into a strict religious rite. The "uncleanness" resulting from the shedding of blood was transformed into spiritual impurity, which required some form of ritual expiation.

It is not uncommon today to hear people say that the spirit of the slain person will haunt his murderer to the grave. Such is the tenacity of a superstition.

Even the blood upon the garment of the warrior made him *taboo* until purified. It was the fear that the

[9] I *Chronicles* 28, vs. 2 and 3.

blood of those killed might be carried within the camp and their spirits wreak vengeance on the tribe that made purification necessary. That is why the stain of blood had to be purged "by fire" and "purified with the waters of separation": [10]

> 22 Only the gold, and the silver, the brass, the iron, the tin, and the lead,
> 23 Every thing that may abide the fire, ye shall make *it* go through the fire, and it shall be clean: nevertheless it shall be purified with the water of separation: and all that abideth not the fire ye shall make go through the water.
> 24 And ye shall wash your clothes on the seventh day, and ye shall be clean, and afterward ye shall come into the camp.

It is also believed that the blood of the slain is supposed to act as a physical poison, should the guilty one communicate with the tribe of the slain.

Another significant Biblical passage indicating the ancient belief that blood spilt within the camp would bring retaliation unless proper expiation were made, is recorded in *Deuteronomy* 21, verses 1 to 9: [11]

> If *one* be found slain in the land which the Lord thy God giveth thee to possess it, lying in the field, *and* it be not known who hath slain him:
> 2 Then thy elders and thy judges shall come forth, and they shall measure unto the cities which *are* round about him that is slain:
> 3 And it shall be, *that* the city *which is* next unto the slain man, even the elders of that city shall take a heifer, which hath not been wrought with, *and* which hath not drawn in the yoke;

[10] *Numbers* 31, vs. 22 to 24.

[11] The explanatory caption in the Bible at the beginning of this chapter is significantly stated as "the expiation of an uncertain murder."

4 And the elders of that city shall bring down the heifer unto a rough valley, which is neither eared nor sown, and shall strike off the heifer's neck there in the valley.

5 And the priests the sons of Levi shall come near; for them the Lord thy God hath chosen to minister unto him, and to bless in the name of the Lord; and by their word shall every controversy and every stroke be *tried:*

6 And all the elders of that city, *that are* next unto the slain *man,* shall wash their hands over the heifer that is beheaded in the valley:

7 And they shall answer and say, Our hands have not shed this blood, neither have our eyes seen *it.*

8 Be merciful, O Lord, unto thy people Israel, whom thou hast redeemed, and lay not innocent blood unto thy people of Israel's charge. And the blood shall be forgiven them.

9 So shalt thou put away the *guilt of* innocent blood from among you, when thou shalt do *that which is* right in the sight of the Lord.

It is to be noted that the discovery of the dead man became important because he had been slain and there had been no proper expiation for the blood which had been spilled. Since it was not known who had committed the deed, it was necessary to purge the place nearest to where the man was found. The expiation consisted of killing an innocent heifer "which hath not been wrought with, and which hath not drawn in the yoke. And the elders of that city shall bring down the heifer unto a rough valley, which is neither eared nor sown, and shall strike off the heifer's neck there in the valley."

In addition, ". . . all the elders of that city, that are next unto the slain man, shall wash their hands over the heifer that is beheaded in the valley; and they shall answer and say, Our hands have not shed this blood, neither have our eyes seen it."

Doubly significant is the fact that the slain man's next of kin were obliged to participate in the expiatory ceremonies, so that they might not be victims of the avenging spirit of the slain man's blood. And so, as is the custom in all primitive societies where this belief prevails, the stain of blood had to be removed by some form of expiation, to free the family and the clan from contamination.

In some primitive communities, expiation is effected by sprinkling the perpetrator with the spurted blood of a slain suckling pig.[12] The ceremony of the ancient Hebrews differs only in method. The superstition is the same.

This is another indication of the primitive cultural concept of morals. You cannot "expiate" a murder. Murder is irreparable. The best that can be done is to make amends. No act or acts, prayers or supplication can restore the life of one who is murdered.

That killing the heifer and washing the hands of the elders had absolutely no relationship to the murder of the man or to expiating the crime could not be understood by the ignorant people of Biblical times. Even one who had merely touched the body of a dead person

[12] Westermarck, *Morals,* Vol. I, p. 376.

was unclean and had to be "purified," for "this is the ordinance of the law which the Lord hath commanded." [13]

> 11 He that toucheth the dead body of any man shall be unclean seven days.
> 12 He shall purify himself with it on the third day, and on the seventh day he shall be clean: but if he purify not himself the third day, then the seventh day he shall not be clean.
> 13 Whosoever toucheth the dead body of any man that is dead, and purifieth not himself, defileth the tabernacle of the Lord; and that soul shall be cut off from Israel; because the water of separation was not sprinkled upon him, he shall be unclean; his uncleanness *is* yet upon him.

So strong was the fear of blood pollution that if a man failed to purify himself as provided in the previous verses of this chapter, he "defileth the tabernacle of the Lord," and his "soul shall be cut off from Israel."

Not only was it necessary to purify the garments of all those who had been slain in battle, but everything that might retain the slightest possibility of contamination—"this is the ordinance of the law which the Lord hath commanded." [14]

> 14 This *is* the law, when a man dieth in a tent: all that come into the tent, and all that *is* in the tent, shall be unclean seven days.
> 15 And every open vessel, which hath no covering bound upon it, *is* unclean.

[13] *Numbers* 19, vs. 11 to 13.
[14] *Numbers* 19, vs. 14 and 15.

The following verses reiterate the importance of purification: [15]

> 16 And whosoever toucheth one that is slain with a sword in the open fields, or a dead body, or a bone of a man, or a grave, shall be unclean seven days.
>
> 17 And for an unclean *person* they shall take of the ashes of the burnt heifer of purification for sin, and running water shall be put thereto in a vessel:
>
> 18 And a clean person shall take hyssop, and dip *it* in the water, and sprinkle *it* upon the tent, and upon all the vessels, and upon the persons that were there, and upon him that touched a bone, or one slain, or one dead, or a grave:
>
> 19 And the clean *person* shall sprinkle upon the unclean on the third day, and on the seventh day: and on the seventh day he shall purify himself, and wash his clothes, and bathe himself in water, and shall be clean at even.
>
> 20 But the man that shall be unclean, and shall not purify himself, that soul shall be cut off from among the congregation, because he hath defiled the sanctuary of the Lord; the water of separation hath not been sprinkled upon him; he *is* unclean.
>
> 21 And it shall be a perpetual statute unto them, that he that sprinkleth the water of separation shall wash his clothes; and he that toucheth the water of separation shall be unclean until even.
>
> 22 And whatsoever the unclean *person* toucheth shall be unclean; and the soul that toucheth *it* shall be unclean until even.

No better summary of the explanation of the fear of

[15] *Numbers* 19, vs. 16-22.

blood pollution could be given than by quoting, again: [16]

> 33 So ye shall not pollute the land wherein ye *are:* for blood it defileth the land: and the land cannot be cleansed of the blood that is shed therein, but by the blood of him that shed it.
> 34 Defile not therefore the land which ye shall inhabit, wherein I dwell: for I the Lord dwell among the children of Israel.

The children of Israel were so obsessed with this fear that they were solemnly warned against permitting such defilement to pollute their land, and if they failed to observe the prescribed rites of expiation, they would suffer the consequences: That "the land spue not you out also, when ye defile it, as it spued out the nations that were before you." [17]

Into the category of the "unclean," as a blood-polluting agent and as one capable of defiling others, woman was placed. This taboo upon woman included her days of menstruation, her pregnancy, and a specified time after the birth of her child. It also precluded her from touching "holy" things, from participating in festivals of holy events, and even her children had to be "cleansed" from contact and contamination with her, while the woman herself was perpetually forced to undergo a period of making herself ritually "clean." [18]

---

[16] *Numbers* 35, vs. 33 and 34.
[17] *Leviticus* 18, v. 28. (Hebrew Bible.)
[18] For the prevalence of this belief among other primitive tribes, see Frazer, *Folklore in the Old Testament*, pp. 33 to 36.

How, it might be asked, could such a belief in blood contamination be responsible for the mutilating rite of circumcision? For substantiation of this practice, the Bible itself furnishes the evidence.

Chapter II

CIRCUMCISION A BLOOD ATONEMENT

IN THE PREVIOUS CHAPTER we quoted Biblical testimony as proof that the belief in blood pollution was one of the deeply-rooted superstitions of the Children of Israel.

In this chapter, Biblical testimony will be adduced as proof that the act of circumcision was a blood atonement, due to the belief prevalent in primitive Hebrew culture that woman herself was a polluting instrument, and of the necessity of avoiding the evil consequences that would follow contact with her.

Her own child became a victim of her "uncleanness."

This act of primitive savagery became one of the most important rituals in the religious conduct of the Children of Israel.

Here are the facts: [1]

> 19 And if a woman have an issue, *and* her issue in her flesh be blood, she shall be put apart seven days: and whosoever toucheth her shall be unclean until the even.

[1] *Leviticus* 15, vs. 19 to 28.

20 And every thing that she lieth upon in her separation shall be unclean: every thing also that she sitteth upon shall be unclean.

21 And whosoever toucheth her bed shall wash his clothes, and bathe *himself* in water, and be unclean until the even.

22 And whosoever toucheth any thing that she sat upon shall wash his clothes, and bathe *himself* in water, and be unclean until the even.

23 And if it *be* on *her* bed, or on any thing whereon she sitteth, when he toucheth it, he shall be unclean until the even.

24 And if any man lie with her at all, and her flowers be upon him, he shall be unclean seven days; and all the bed whereon he lieth shall be unclean.

25 And if a woman have an issue of her blood many days out of the time of her separation, or if it run beyond the time of her separation; all the days of the issue of her uncleanness shall be as the days of her separation: she *shall be* unclean.

26 Every bed whereon she lieth all the days of her issue shall be unto her as the bed of her separation: and whatsoever she sitteth upon shall be unclean, as the uncleanness of her separation.

27 And whosoever toucheth those things shall be unclean, and shall wash his clothes, and bathe *himself* in water, and be unclean until the even.

28 But if she be cleansed of her issue, then she shall number to herself seven days, and after that she shall be clean.

Let me repeat the significant words of this Biblical quotation: ". . . If a woman have an issue, *and* her issue in her flesh be blood [menstruation], she shall be put apart seven days, and *whosoever* toucheth her shall be unclean . . ." (italics mine).

The woman's "uncleanness" was not meant in an unhygienic sense. If that were true, the mere *washing* would be sufficient to make her *clean* again; but washing and "uncleanness" were not synonymous words in Biblical times. Her purification came about because "she shall be put apart for seven days," to become ritually clean before the danger of contamination with her was removed.

Not only must she be purified from her "uncleanness" but ". . . everything that she lieth upon . . . everything also that she sitteth upon shall be unclean. . . . And whosoever toucheth her bed . . . and whosoever toucheth anything that she sat upon . . . shall . . . be unclean . . ."

Such was the terrifying belief in the contamination from the issue of the blood of woman which prevailed among the Children of Israel in early Biblical times. And so the cycle of "uncleanness" and the ceremony of "purification" continued month after month and year after year. It was the eternal torment of every household.

The word "unclean," as Biblically used, had a ritual meaning and was never intended to mean *unclean* in the modern sense of the word; that is, physically or hygienically.[2] The highest Biblical and Hebrew authorities admit that such was its original meaning. To be *unclean* was to be *taboo*.

In view of this great dread, what must the woman do to make herself "clean" again and to make her household and all those who dwelt therein ritually acceptable in the sight of their god? Here is the formula, and note well its "hygienic" association:[3]

[2] See *New Standard Bible Dictionary*.
[3] *Leviticus* 15, vs. 29 to 31.

29 And on the eighth day she shall take
unto her two turtles, or two young
pigeons, and bring them unto the priest,
to the door of the tabernacle of the
congregation.

30 And the priest shall offer the one
for a sin offering, and the other *for* a
burnt offering; and the priest shall make
an atonement for her before the Lord
for the issue of her uncleanness.

31 Thus shall ye separate the children
of Israel from their uncleanness; that
they die not in their uncleanness, when
they defile my tabernacle that *is* among
them.

As a final expiation for her "uncleanness," ". . . she
shall take unto her two turtles, or two young pigeons,
and bring them unto the priest . . . and he shall offer
the one *for* a sin offering, and shall offer the other *for* a
burnt offering; and the priest shall make *an atonement*
(italics mine) for her before the Lord for the issue of
her uncleanness."

An atonement for what?

What sin is there in being a woman?

Is not her task in life difficult enough as it is, *because
she is a woman,* without placing the additional stigma
of "sin" upon her?

What monstrous perversity lies behind this conception?

What possible connection is there in the killing of
two innocent and harmless forms of life as a sacrifice
for so valueless a purpose? By the wildest stretch of
the imagination, no relationship whatever can be associated with a woman's "uncleanness" and the killing of

two turtles in expiation for a perfectly natural function of her body.

For the penalty of having become a mother, she was forced to make an additional blood sacrifice by offering a lamb to be slaughtered.[4]

Nor is there in this sacrifice, brutal and bloody though it be, any magic formula that will "separate the Children of Israel from their uncleanness," nor that will prevent the "defilement" of the tabernacle of the Lord.

Nor does this act have the remotest association in any manner, shape or form, with hygienic conditions. It is solely a savage sacrifice of blood as an expiation because of the superstitious fear of blood pollution.

For the purpose of this study, I wish to quote again the warning contained in verse 10, that "whosoever toucheth her shall be unclean." The significance of this statement and its relationship with circumcision will follow shortly.

This primitive superstition concerning the sexual function of woman was made part of the ritual and law of the Children of Israel. Her physical condition was looked upon as a curse from God, and fear of contamination became an obsession. Naturally, a menstruous woman was taboo on the Sabbath. Not only was everything she touched made "unclean," but "everything that she lieth upon . . . everything that she sitteth upon . . . whoever toucheth her bed . . . whoever toucheth anything that she sat upon . . . shall be

[4] *Leviticus* 12, vs. 6 to 8.

THE TABOOED WOMAN

unclean." Under such conditions, how could she possibly participate in the observance of so sacred a day as the Sabbath without "polluting" it?[5]

Since it was obviously impossible for any woman to avoid her "uncleanness" on the Sabbath, she was forbidden to participate in observing this sacred day solely to prevent its contamination by her. "Ye shall separate the Children of Israel from their uncleanness . . . unless . . . they defile my tabernacle."

Even the Talmud refers to the *taboo* associated with a menstruating woman and the dread in which she is held while in that condition. It is related that when a woman meets a snake on the road, it is enough for her to say, "I am menstruating," and the reptile will glide away hastily. According to the Talmud, if a woman at the beginning of her period passes between two men, she causes one of them to die; if she passes between them at the end of her period, she only causes them to quarrel violently.

This belief about a menstruous woman was not confined to the early and uncultured Hebrew; it prevailed in many societies and is mentioned in many "sacred" books.

The Persian lawgiver, Zoroaster, who claimed to have received his code direct from the mouth of the Supreme Being, Ahura Mazda, said that a menstruous woman is the work of Ahriman, the devil. Therefore,

[5] See the author's analysis of the Fourth Commandment in his book, *The Ten Commandments,* on this subject as to the reason why woman was not included in the observance of the Sabbath.

while a woman is in that condition, she is unclean and possessed of the demon; she must be kept apart from the faithful whom her touch would defile. The Zoroastrian religious books enter into minute details. The very glance of a menstruous woman was regarded as polluting anything upon which it fell. Hence, a menstruating woman must not look upon a fire, or upon water, or converse with any man. No fire was to be kindled in the house during that period.[6]

Similar superstitions, too numerous to mention, prevail among all types of people. The superstition still prevails today that a living plant will wither at the touch of a menstruous woman, and that women during that period should not make food preserves of any kind, as they would spoil.

After recounting instances of this taboo and their purificatory rites for a menstruous woman, as well as a woman in childbirth, Frazer [7] concludes with this observation: "These customs show that in the opinion of some primitive peoples, a woman at and after childbirth is pervaded by a certain dangerous influence which can infect anything and anybody she touches, so that, in the interest of the community, it becomes necessary to seclude her from society for a while until the virulence of the infection has passed away, when, after submitting to certain rites of purification, she is again free to mingle with her fellows."

[6] For the widespread prevalence of this belief, see Briffault, *The Mothers,* Vol. II, p. 370.
[7] *Taboo and The Perils of the Soul,* p. 150.

So widespread was this superstition, and so firmly was it believed, that even members of the medical profession fell under its influence.

As late as 1878, a physician wrote to the editor of the *British Medical Journal,* asking him whether a ham cured by a menstruating woman would be spoiled! Not until 1891 did Doctor William Goodell, a distinguished medical authority, state, "I have learned to unlearn the teaching that women must not be subjected to a surgical operation during her monthly flux. Our forefathers, from time immemorial, have thought and taught that the presence of a menstruating woman would pollute solemn religious rites, would sour milk, spoil the fermentation of wine-vats, and do much other mischief in a general way. . . ." [8]

If the purpose of circumcision is hygienic, as some maintain, then why was it not mentioned for this purpose in the following Biblical text in which God is supposed to have laid down the law of circumcision to Moses? [9]

> 9 And God said unto Abraham, Thou shalt keep my covenant therefore, thou, and thy seed after thee in their generations.
> 10 This *is* my covenant, which ye shall keep, between me and you and thy seed after thee; Every man child among you shall be circumcised.
> 11 And ye shall circumcise the flesh of your foreskin; and it shall be a token of the covenant betwixt me and you.

[8] Havelock Ellis, *Psychology of Sex,* Vol. I, p. 293. See also Haggard, *Devils, Drugs and Doctors.*

[9] *Genesis* 17, vs. 9 to 14.

> 12 And he that is eight days old shall be circumcised among you, every man child in your generations, he that is born in the house, or bought with money of any stranger, which *is* not of thy seed.
> 13 He that is born in thy house, and he that is bought with thy money, must needs be circumcised: and my covenant shall be in your flesh for an everlasting covenant.
> 14 And the uncircumcised man child whose flesh of his foreskin is not circumcised, that soul shall be cut off from his people; he hath broken my covenant.

These verses specifically and unequivocally state that "circumcision shall be a token of the covenant betwixt me and you," not a word even remotely suggesting health or hygiene!

Since the mother, during her thirty-three day period of purification must, of necessity, touch her child, what must be done to save him from the pollution caused by his contact with her?

The required mode of expiation, as contained in verse 11, just quoted, provides that: "And in the eighth day the flesh of his foreskin shall be circumcised."

Let me again state with emphasis that *this ritual injunction, following the birth of a male child, and its direct relation to the mother's state of taboo, is a blood sacrifice on behalf of the boy to avoid the contamination of having come into contact with the mother's "uncleanness."*

This *taboo* upon woman has undoubtedly been the cause of the restrictions placed upon her, not only in association with "holy" things, but in excluding her from the fields of the learned professions. But progress is being made, for today there are women physicians!

When a person is *taboo,* the *taboo* applies not only to that person but also to everything he or she touches. If food that a menstruous woman touches is unfit for a man to eat, how much more serious is her association with "sacred" things, and how much more important is it that she be prevented from polluting them!

It is very important that this primitive conception of woman's position be understood in order to obtain a proper comprehension of the reason for her being *tabooed.*

As previously stated, pregnancy and childbirth also placed woman in the category of a *taboo* person and called for a ritual expiation of her "sinful" condition.

The Biblical Hebrews distinguished between the birth of a male and a female child by providing a different form of expiation, and in carefully examining this, we come upon the secret of male circumcision.[10]

> And the Lord spake unto Moses, saying,
> 2 Speak unto the children of Israel, saying, If a woman have conceived seed, and borne a man child, then she shall be unclean seven days; according to the days of the separation for her infirmity shall she be unclean.
> 3 And in the eighth day the flesh of his foreskin shall be circumcised.
> 4 And she shall then continue in the blood of her purifying three and thirty days; she shall touch no hallowed thing, nor come into the sanctuary, until the days of her purifying be fulfilled.

So vitally important was this blood expiation on be-

[10] *Leviticus* 12, vs. 1 to 4.

half of the child that the rite of circumcision had to be performed on the eighth day after its birth, even though that day fell on the Sabbath. This precluded others from doing it, making it necessary for the mother herself to perform the task.[11]

This blood sacrifice, so obvious when understood in relation to the *taboo* of women and the primitive Hebrew's belief in blood pollution, reveals the secret of the origin and meaning of the ceremonial rite of circumcision among the Children of Israel.

The origin and reason for circumcision have puzzled anthropologists and students of religion for centuries. The highest Biblical authorities still tell us that the rite of circumcision among the Children of Israel is one of the mysteries of Judaism, as its origin has been lost in antiquity. There seems to be no doubt that this rite originated in the remotest past, as the first Biblical reference to it mentions that circumcision was performed with sharp stones, the most primitive cutting instrument used by man. This rough and crude instrument was used because of the necessity for shedding blood as a result of the operation.[12] If no blood came from the cutting of the prepuce, then a token of blood was taken from another part of the body.

Even the correct meaning of the word "circumcision," both in Arabic and Hebrew, is "purifying," as well as "removing a sexual obstacle" and "cleansing,"

[11] *Jewish Encyclopedia,* Vol. 4, p. 95.
[12] *Ibid.,* Vol. IV, p. 95

in a religious sense. That "purification" in a ritual sense was the purpose [13] of circumcision cannot be doubted, in view of the indisputable facts here recorded.

That this sacrificial expiation of blood atonement prevailed among other primitive tribes obsessed by savage superstition, needs but a few examples to indicate its prevalence, although the method varied from merely slitting the prepuce to its complete removal. Many and various customs have been associated with it. Among the East African Wakikuyu the prepuce is buried in the ground in front of the boy just circumcised; while the African Bara father throws it into the river. For fear of its being used in black magic, the Turks bury the prepuce as they do parings of nails and other parts of the body. For a similar reason, the Amaxosa Kafir boy carries away his prepuce and buries it in a sacred spot.

On the West Coast of Africa, the prepuce, soaked in brandy, is swallowed by the boy operated upon. The Arabs of Algiers wrap it in a cloth and put it on a tree or animal. The Hova of Madagascar wrap it in a banana leaf which is given to a calf to eat. Among the Wolof, the prepuce is dried and is carried by the circumcised lad, the object being the promotion of virility. Today, among the Sakalava of Madagascar, the foreskin is shot from a gun or fastened to a spear; if it falls sticking in the earth, it is a good omen.

[13] *Exodus* 4, v. 25.

The ceremonial rite of circumcision among the Kiuyu consists of preparations the day before circumcision takes place. A he-goat is killed by being strangled, its skin cut into strips and fastened around the wrist and carried over the back of the male.

Among the Washamba, another tribe of East Africa, a goat is sacrificed to an ancestral spirit.

In a similar ceremony, the Bworana Gallas gathered with parents and relatives into a hut. A bullock is then killed as a sacrifice, and each person present dips a finger into the blood which is allowed to flow over the ground; the men daub the blood on their foreheads and the women on their windpipes.[14]

Among some Mohammedan tribes, the bridegroom is circumcised on the day after his marriage, and sprinkles the blood that falls from the penis onto the veil of the bride. However, the circumcision does not stop with the removal of the prepuce. The ceremony is one of endurance, while the wife watches the performance. The man submits himself to the priest of the holy office. After the prepuce is removed, the next procedure is to remove the skin from the whole organ.

Regardless of what our reaction is to this frightful and inhuman act, if the victim should show the slightest emotion of pain or exhibit any sign of weakness, such as a sigh or a groan, the bride leaves him, saying that she does not want such a weakling for a husband!

14 Frazer, *loc. cit.,* pp. 210 to 211.

It is needless to say that a large proportion of bridegrooms die from such an operation.[15]

Some form of blood expiation and mutilation prevailed among the primitive Mexicans. While they practised circumcision as we know it today, they also resorted to the cutting off of the ear as a means of blood expiation. This, however, was abandoned, and the circumcision was modified to that of only bleeding the prepuce and making an incision in the ear.

They also practiced, as part of the same rite, the deflowering of young girls. This was generally done by the priest who used his finger for that purpose.[16]

Among some Australians, the initiation custom prevailing at circumcision is: the boy is lifted up and above two men, and some of the blood is allowed to drip down on their backs, as a bond establishing a special friendly relationship between himself and them.[17]

Among the Caribs, they sprinkle a male infant with his father's blood to give him some of his father's courage.

Among the Australian Urabunja, the stomach of each elder brother is touched with the foreskin, which is then placed on a fire stick and buried.[18]

The northern Arunta bury the prepuce together with

---

[15] Remondino, *Circumcision*, p. 55.
[16] *Ibid.*, pp. 46, 47.
[17] Hastings, *Encyclopedia of Religion and Ethics*, Vol. 2, p. 715.
[18] *Ibid.*, Vol. 3, p. 600.

the blood caused by the operation. The Kalkodoon of Cloninny (North Queensland) string it on a twine of human hair and hang it around the mother's neck "to keep the devil away." The Anula bury it beside a pool to make the water lilies grow. Among the Yaro-inga of the Upper Georgina District, the blood shed in circumcision is drunk by the women of the tribe as a strengthening draught.[19]

In some Australian tribes, boys who are being circumcised are laid on a platform formed by the living bodies of the tribesmen. The boy's tooth is knocked out as an initiatory ceremony. He is then seated on the shoulders of a man on whose breast the blood flows and may not be wiped away.[20]

And to think that this bloody ritual of savage superstition survives today under the guise of a health and hygienic measure!

If circumcision is the expiatory rite for the birth of a male child who comes in contact with the mother's "uncleanness," what shall be done as a sacrifice for a "maid child?" The Bible tells us: [21]

> 5 But if she bear a maid child, then she shall be unclean two weeks, as in her separation; and she shall continue in the blood of her purifying threescore and six days.

Although female circumcision was practiced among

[19] *Ibid.,* Vol. 3, p. 662.
[20] Frazer, *The Golden Bough,* p. 229.
[21] *Leviticus* 12, v. 5.

primitive tribes, it is now rarely performed.[22] This may be due to the fact that the genital organs of the female infant do not permit such an operation as easily as that performed on the male, and when done by unskilled hands, it is likely to result in the death of the child.[23]

The mother was not only unclean two weeks instead of one week, but "she shall continue in the blood of her purifying *threescore and six days*"—a period twice as long as that for the male child.

Equally important, in regard to the *taboo,* is the method of expiation for the mother's own state of blood pollution. The Bible reveals the method she must follow "when her days of purifying are fulfilled." [24]

> 6 And when the days of her purifying are fulfilled, for a son, or for a daughter, she shall bring a lamb of the first year for a burnt offering, and a young pigeon, or a turtledove, for a sin offering, unto the door of the tabernacle of the congregation, unto the priest:
> 7 Who shall offer it before the Lord, and make an atonement for her; and she shall be cleansed from the issue of her blood. This *is* the law for her that hath borne a male or a female.
> 8 And if she be not able to bring a lamb, then she shall bring two turtles, or two young pigeons; the one for the burnt offering, and the other for a sin offering: and the priest shall make an atonement for her, and she shall be clean.

What better parallel can be drawn than that which

[22] When a female was circumcised, it was done at puberty, and consisted in cutting off the nymphae, or labia minora, of the vulva, which unite over the clitoris.

[23] For the prevalence of female circumcision, see Hastings, *loc. cit.,* Vol. 3, pp. 667-668.

[24] *Leviticus* 12, vs. 6 to 8.

BLOOD ATONEMENT

existed between the uncultured, primitive Hebrew and the ignorant people of Bokhara? In Bokhara the mother of a child is *taboo* for forty days, and does not even dare to pray to God while her supposed impurity lasts! [25]

How similar to the Bible are the provisions in the sacred book of the Zend-Avesta for the purification of women after childbirth! Not only must a woman's clothes all be burned after her ordeal, but she must be purified by being washed with bull's urine.[26] Her *taboo* lasted forty days, and anyone attempting to break this *taboo* was severely punished as guilty of the most unspeakable crime. Nyan women are similarly regarded at such times. After confinement, they must not enter a sacred place for forty days.[27] A woman in this state is supposed to be possessed by some dangerous and malevolent spirit that corrupts all with which she comes in contact.

Among the Yukaghir, a woman is *taboo* after childbirth and must be careful not to touch any hunting or fishing instrument. A Koryak woman after childbirth is *taboo* and her touch will deprive a shaman's drum of its virtue; she must not even be seen by any one.

Among the Gilyak, a woman never dares to give birth to a child at home; she must, in spite of the severity of season or weather, go out of the hut for the purpose. The women of Kamchatka are under obligation to

[25] Briffault, *loc. cit.,* Vol. 2, p. 374.
[26] *Ibid.,* p. 376.
[27] *Ibid.,* p. 378.

leave their huts when about to give birth to a child, which is born in the public street of the village before the populace.[28]

Among the Samoyeds and the Ostyak, women at childbirth may not eat any fresh meat for fear that living animals would be affected, and in order to insure against all possible risks they must not, even at ordinary times, stand over the reindeer while unloading a sledge, but must undo the straps from below.

Among the Basutos the father is separated from the mother and child for four days after birth, and he may not see them until the "medicine man" has performed the religious ceremony of "absolution of the man and wife." If this were neglected, it is believed that he would die when he saw his wife.

Women in Russia, before the present regime, were considered in a state of impurity after childbirth, and were not permitted to communicate with others until they had been purified by a priest. In Serbia, similar conditions prevailed. Among the Tibetan tribes of Lab Nor, a mother is driven from the village in which she lives and is compelled to live in a near-by hut or along the roadside. Food is supplied to her by the husband.[29]

Frazer truly says, ". . . there may survive not a few savage *taboos* which, masquerading as an expression of the divine will . . . have maintained their credit long after the crude ideas out of which they sprang have

[28] *Ibid.*, pp. 373-374.
[29] Briffault, *loc. cit.*, Vol. 2, pp. 373-419.

been discarded by the progress of thought and knowledge." [30]

If women had to be *purified* ritually in early Biblical
times for having given birth, what change has taken
place that makes such a ceremony no longer necessary?

The same liberating force of scientific knowledge
that has emancipated us from other forms of religious
superstition and fear is responsible for breaking these
taboos that have so long enslaved women.

Now that women are no longer forced to observe this
savage custom of "purification," nor condemned to
suffer for the "sin" of uncleanness, circumcising male
children as a blood atonement cannot be characterized
as anything but a cruel mutilation and the survival of
a savage custom.

[30] *The Taboo and the Perils of the Soul,* p. 218.

Chapter III

THE RITE OF CIRCUMCISION

THIS RITUAL of circumcision has become so deeply in-grained in the mind of the Hebrew as a prerequisite of his religious and racial solidarity, that no matter how lax he may be in observing the other rituals of his religion, he will not fail to observe this one. He considers it an all-important act not only of piety but as an essential requirement in complying with the "commands" of his God.

His unfailing observance of this ritual springs not only from the fact that he considers it an act of devotion to his religion but from the belief that it possesses some kind of magic power that will save him from the wrath of his jealous God.[1]

Does not the text specifically state that "he that is born in the house . . . must needs be circumcised: and my covenant shall be in his flesh [blood sacrifice and atonement] for an everlasting covenant . . . lest his soul shall be cut off from his people. . . ."

Is there any element of health and hygiene in this

[1] *Jewish Encyclopedia*, Vol. 4, p. 92.

THE CEREMONY OF CIRCUMCISION

command? On the contrary, it was a warning that unless he fulfilled the covenant he would be ostracized from Hebrew society, which meant a fate worse than death.

Can there be any doubt, in view of these facts, that health and hygiene have no relationship to this act whatsoever?

In Hebrew literature it is taught that "Israel was redeemed from Egypt because of a double blood merit, the blood of the Paschal lamb and the blood of circumcision; and Israel 'shall take of the blood and put it on the lintel' of their houses as a token that the Destroyer shall not have power over their homes to do them harm." [2]

In consequence, all the children who "came out of Egypt" were circumcised, but those "born in the wilderness" were not; and, "therefore, Joshua, before the celebration of the Passover, had them circumcised with knives of flint (compare *Exodus* 4, verse 25) at Gilgal, which name is explained as the 'rolling away' of the reproach of Egypt."

So essential was the rite of circumcision, that because Moses failed to circumcise his first-born, the Lord "sought to kill him," whereupon Zipporah, his wife, took a flint and cut off the foreskin of her son and cast it at Moses' feet, saying, "A bridegroom of blood art thou to me." [3]

And so circumcision became the supreme act of loy-

---

[2] *Exodus* 12, v. 7; also, Trachtenberg, *Jewish Magic and Superstitution,* p. 170.

[3] *Exodus* 4, vs. 24 to 26. Also, *Jewish Encyclopedia,* Vol. 4, p. 92.

alty to the Hebrew Deity and a mark of solidarity to the Children of Israel.[4]

The Hebrew scholar, Joshua Trachtenberg, in his extremely valuable book, *Jewish Magic and Superstition,* very rightly considers circumcision as a magical rite and as a protection against the forces of evil, in the same way as magic wands and amulets are now used either to bring good luck or to ward off harm.

Circumcision ushered the child into the community of the Children of Israel. This was a most critical time, potent with the forces of evil. During the eight days prior to the operation, both mother and child were in constant danger from "evil" spirits.

These were immediately dissipated after circumcision, as this blood sacrifice was considered sufficient to drive off the evil spirits and at the same time "evoke the guardianship of the powers of good."

One method of accomplishing this result was to place the bloody foreskin in a bowl containing water and spices, and as each member of the congregation left the ceremony, he would bathe his hands and face in it. Another method of producing a "wonderful charm" was that during the days preceding the rite, the foreskin of a child previously circumcised was put into the mouth of one who was to undergo the operation.[5]

This was to bring him benefits from the "good" spirits, despite the danger of spreading disease, a practice which, I believe, belongs in the category of the unhygienic. It is still believed by the orthodox Hebrew

[4] *Jewish Encyclopedia,* Vol. 4, p. 93.
[5] Trachtenberg, *loc. cit.,* p. 170.

that if he is circumcised, all the blessings of God will
fall upon him.

The modern American Jew continues the practice
of circumcision merely because of the power of convention, without the slightest thought or knowledge of
why it is done or the reason for it.

There is another custom that takes place at the time
of circumcision which offers additional evidence that
it originally was and still is a magical rite, and not in
the slightest degree associated with health and hygiene.
This custom is to set aside a chair for the Prophet
Elijah. The legend is that God had rewarded this
prophet for his zealous defense of this rite with the
promise that he would be present at the circumcision
of every child of Israel. During the Middle Ages, it
was customary for the assembled guests to rise before
the ceremony and to greet the unseen visitor with the
words: "Blessed be he that cometh." [6]

Another instance that circumcision was associated
with a propitiatory rite with magical results was the
use of lights as a protective measure during the ceremony. On the days before the circumcision, candles
were lit in profusion, and especially while the act was
being performed. It was believed that no evil could
come to the house while the candles were lit and mysti-
cal prayers were being recited. Some went so far as to
start a vigil the night before to prevent the evil spirits
from interfering with the religious rite of circumcision,
because they believed that circumcision possessed some

[6] Trachtenberg, *loc. cit.*, p. 171.

sort of magic power to save the child from the torments of life and to bring to him the "blessing of God." [7]

So potent did they consider these magical acts, and particularly those associated with the circumcised child, that on the death of the Mohel, or Circumciser, the foreskins of the children he had circumcised were sometimes buried with him to drive away the demons and destroyers who would seek to do him harm after death.[8]

It is also commonly believed by the orthodox that some form of magic prevails over those who have circumcised a certain number of children. This is supposed to prevent putrefaction of their mouths, as well as to prevent their mouths from becoming food for worms after their deaths!!

The belief that circumcision is a ritual possessing magical results has gripped the Jew with an extreme religious fanaticism, and this is borne out by the following quotation from the *Midrash,* one of the most authoritative and sacred Hebrew books: "If thy sons accept my Godhead (by undergoing circumcision), I shall be their God and bring them into the land; but if they do not observe my covenant in regard to either circumcision or to the Sabbath, they shall not enter the land of promise." [9]

The observance of the rite of circumcision has been just about as beneficial to the Jews as has been the observance of the Sabbath. And, of course, there is a

[7] *Ibid.,* p. 170.
[8] *Jewish Encyclopedia,* Vol. 4, p. 95.
[9] *Ibid.,* Vol. 4, p. 95.

direct connection between the two observances, as we have previously shown. In fact, so important did they consider circumcision as a purifying rite, that in order that no one whom they considered unclean might profane the clan, the expiatory rite was even performed upon their servants, as a precautionary measure to prevent evil from being visited upon their tribe. This is how deeply rooted was the fear of failure to observe the rite of blood atonement, because in the mind of the primitive Hebrew, circumcision was "an indispensable act of national consecration and purification, as was the observance of the Sabbath." [10]

It must be understood that when used in a religious sense, the words "consecration and purification" mean "to be holy," and free from any taint of contamination that would profane things considered sacred, and had nothing whatever to do with hygiene as understood today.

Things "unholy" and acts that were considered in violation of this ritual were condemned because they would provoke their jealous and wrathful God to wreak evil upon them. And not only upon the individual violators, but upon the whole tribe, such was the nature of their nationalistic religion and tribal solidarity.

In fact, when considered in the broader aspects of modern intelligence, circumcision has about the same "health and hygienic" value as the *Hollekreisch* which is a magical ceremony used by orthodox Hebrews when

[10] *Ibid.,* p. 92.

naming the child for the purpose of driving off evil spirits. This was accomplished by shouting and tossing the infant in the air! [11]

Those parents who permit their children to be indiscriminately circumcised are in reality merely practising one of the savage rites and ceremonies of primitive Judaism and are guilty of violating the very first essentials of health and hygiene.

[11] Trachtenberg, *loc. cit.*, p. 172.

Chapter IV

"HEALTH" AND "HYGIENE"

THE INTRODUCTION of circumcision in western civilization stems directly from its practice among the Biblical Hebrews. Since Christianity was founded upon the Hebrew Bible, and many of its savage and primitive practices were adopted at its inception, the wonder is that circumcision is not even more widespread than it is.

In fact, the Sabbath and many of Christianity's rituals and ceremonies were copied *in toto* from the Hebrew religion. Despite the fact that the Sabbath was changed from the "seventh" day of the week to the "first"; that many of the ceremonies were camouflaged in new dress, and the ritual procedure changed and supplemented with additional incantations, the fact remains that the pattern is based upon Judaic superstitions.

And superstition, like some diseases, is contagious.

To avoid contamination, one must be forever vigilant.

Health measures for the mind are fully as important as health measures for the body.

Knowledge is the antidote to protect the former, just as cleanliness is the antidote to protect the latter.

The poison of superstition affects the mind and often proves just as fatal as the contagious diseases that attack the body. The history of progress offers innumerable examples.

As, for instance,

The Decalogue's prohibition against the making of "graven images," with the result that its observance was responsible for paralyzing for nearly three thousand years the artistic instinct in the Hebrew people;

The belief that disease was sent as a punishment for sin; and, as a direct result of this mental affliction, practically no progress was made in medicine or science during the Middle Ages; and,

The fanatical fundamentalist's opposition to the teaching of evolution, and the closing of his mind to the truths of science.[1]

Were not the rationalistic and scientific approaches to a problem superior to the dogmatic there would be no progress. Science seeks both the truth and its utilitarianism, while dogmatism not only precludes change, but on the contrary seeks excuses for, and invents explanations, in support of its superstitious practices in the face of undeniable truth.

While the former welcomes investigation, the latter rebels against the slightest questioning of its practices.

[1] For additional material see Drapers' *Conflict between Religion and Science;* White's *Warfare between Science and Theology;* Joseph Lewis, *The Ten Commandments.*

Superstition persists and persists and persists . . . a continuous and never-ending repetition; while science is forever investigating and experimenting in search for the goal of truth that it seeks. Ignorance is doggedly persistent while truth is amazingly patient.

Once the superstitious aspects of his conduct have been exposed the religious believer seeks a rational explanation in justification, and if possible, a plausible excuse for its continuance.

The reasons and excuses advanced today for circumcision by those who still practice it, are so at variance with its original intent and purpose that their explanations would be ludicrous, were not the results so tragic.

This fanatical defense is particularly evident when the act is exposed as a fundamental tenet of religion; then the most fantastic claims are made to justify its practice, and the most outlandish reasons are invented for its observance.

In fact, religionists tell us that the failure to observe these ridiculous practices is considered an insult to God.

What health and hygienic value is there when a child who is born dead must, according to Hebrew Law, be circumcised at the grave before burial?[2] And for the same reason a child born without a prepuce must of necessity go through the ceremony of circumcision, and a few drops of blood must be taken from another part of his body, in order that he might be cleansed of the "impurity" of blood pollution.

[2] *Laws and Customs of Israel,* Vol. I, p. 186, Vol. II, p. 185.

In the first instance, of what value is a "health and hygienic" measure to a child who is *already dead?* And, in the other instance, if the existence of the prepuce contributes to an unhealthy condition, then why, if a child should happen to be born without it, the necessity of insisting that it shed blood from another part of its body?

Because "health and hygiene" have absolutely nothing whatever to do with circumcision. It is performed solely as a fulfillment of the "blood of the Covenant," and *for no other reason.*

The original purpose of circumcision, now revealed as a blood atonement, is too ridiculous for acceptance by the modern world. Its believers, therefore, and those who have come under the spell of this superstition, seek justification for its practice and continuance by explaining that its purpose is "health and hygiene."

It is done for no such purpose. If circumcision is performed "for health and hygienic" reasons, then why not adopt and practice other acts proved by scientific demonstration to actually have health and hygienic value?

If health and hygiene were the real motivating reasons for the practice of circumcision, then how do those who adopt it account for their failure to adopt these other measures which have all the benefits of health and hygiene without the questionable value and the dangers of circumcision? Why do they continually persist in indulging in acts that are so glaringly and flagrantly inimical to health and hygiene?

Health authorities will tell you how difficult it is to get people to practice health and hygienic measures that have been proved beyond question as to their value and importance, such as, the eating of natural brown rice in preference to polished rice, whole wheat bread in preference to bread made from bleached white flour, fresh fruits and vegetables in preference to foods adulterated with poisonous preservatives, and other measures too numerous to mention.

There is an old expression to the effect that when a religious person is asked why he inflicts upon himself so many burdensome acts of observance, he replies that he is only sorry there are not more such acts which he could suffer so as to demonstrate the greater proof of his faith.

Such is the fanaticism induced by religion.

Into this category belongs the blind acceptance of circumcision. And its spread and adoption by others is not based upon any logical reason or proven value but merely because it is but another act in the silly and sometimes fatal rites in the catalogue of superstitious conduct.

Sometimes, the more humiliating the act, the more readily it is practised as a demonstration of one's "love of God," and the more religious one is the more susceptible he is to adopt such conduct—though it be fantastic in the extreme—as evidence of his religious devotion.

That is why many Catholics and Protestants today have permitted their children to be circumcised, and this acceptance by them has been given as proof that it has "health and hygienic" value.

By what formula of magic can the superstitious rites of one religion, when accepted by a believer in another religion, turn that superstition into values ever so remotely removed from it?

Before the Catholic or Protestant believer can claim that he has adopted circumcision for its health and hygienic value, he must first explain what health and hygienic value his own superstitious observances possess that makes him, because of his adoption of circumcision, an authority in that department of medicine.

Imitation may be the sincerest form of flattery but flattery is a poor substitute for hygienic precaution.

Professor Charles Richet [3] denounces this claim for circumcision in these words: "Sometimes an attempt is made to justify circumcision by saying that it is a measure of hygiene and cleanliness. What! must a man have a scrap of his skin cut off in order to be clean? Are Christians therefore condemned never to be as clean as Jews? Absurd! Amazingly absurd! Homo Stultissimus!"

The suggested use of soap and water is not an insulting recommendation, and, in addition, it is unquestionably warranted to be definitely hygienic.

[3] *Idiot Man,* p. 26.

Chapter V

IS CIRCUMCISION A MEDICAL PROBLEM?

WHEN THE QUESTION of circumcision is discussed, the opinion generally advanced by those who have given the subject *no* consideration is that "it is a medical problem."

Such a statement is an indication of the ignorance which prevails concerning this important matter.

Circumcision is not a medical problem. It becomes one only after the child has been circumcised in conformity with the religious ceremony, because he then needs the attention of a trained and experienced physician to save him from the dangers that are present following the completion of this savage rite.

The circumcised child has undergone an operation by one wholly unqualified for such a "job," which may and often does have serious consequences.

If the rite of circumcision is a medical problem, why is it performed as a religious ceremony by one who is not a physician?

Among the orthodox Hebrews, this ceremony is called the "Brith Milah," and is performed by the Circumciser, generally a Mohel or a Rabbi, one especially delegated to perform the ceremony because of his specific training for this particular religious act.

If circumcision is a medical problem, then why is it performed by one religiously trained in all its ritual details and who is totally unfamiliar with its medical aspects?

In fact, the more "religious" the Circumciser, the more desirable that he be the one to perform the act.

What does the Mohel know about the physiology of the genital organs? He not only does not give the child a physical examination, but does not even possess the medical knowledge required to know whether or not its condition warrants circumcision.

Not only is he ignorant of the medical knowledge necessary to determine whether or not the child requires such an operation, but he is not medically trained to perform it.

In fact, the Circumciser, whether Mohel or Rabbi, is not concerned in the slightest degree whatsoever with the medical aspects of circumcision. He performs the act as a religious rite, irrespective of whether it is warranted or not. The only concern of the Mohel is to carry out, in all its harrowing details, this barbarous act, just as he performs the religious ceremony in the ritual killing of an animal.

And then again, the indiscriminate circumcising of

all Hebrew male children is additional proof that it is not a medical problem, but rather one of a religious rite.

Physicians who attend the delivery of children of non-Hebrew parents, and who are instructed by them to circumcise their children, generally do so as a matter of course. The physician who carries out this request and performs the operation without first acquainting the parents with all the medical facts associated with it is, in my opinion, derelict in his duty, and it is a serious reflection upon his medical ethics.

If circumcision were a medical problem, the new-born infant should be examined by a trained physician *before* the operation to determine whether it is required, and unless there is something unusual or abnormal about the prepuce, no physician can determine on the eighth day, or the eighteenth day, or the eightieth day, for that matter, whether that infant must, of necessity, as a protection to its health, be circumcised.

The truth of the matter is that the great majority of children who are circumcised today undergo this operation without medical advice, and this mutilating act is performed because of its religious significance, despite, and in defiance of, medical disapproval.

The eminent physician and surgeon, Doctor Miles Atkinson, in his recent book, *Behind the Mask of Medicine,* states in emphatic terms and in unequivocal language his opposition and condemnation of circumcision.

The purpose of Doctor Atkinson's researches into the subject was to discover ". . . why the religious rite of one people should have become the common practice of many others, and what justification there is for it when divorced from its religious implications." He takes cognizance of its increase because, he says, "Most parents seem to give no thought to it" and consider it as a matter of course that, being born a boy necessitates being circumcised, as though "it was one of the necessary losses of life" and "better get it over and done with."

In most cases, the child is circumcised simply upon the advice of those who "believe in it" and, sometimes, only because Grandma thinks it is a "good thing."

Doctor Atkinson does not hesitate to say that "it might increase the sum of human happiness if we gave the matter a little more thought" because "very few babies . . . actually require circumcision."

He accounts for its spread among non-Jewish people to thoughtlessness and indifference, and he says that "it seems impossible to avoid the conclusion that the large majority of circumcisions are done, not on any scientific principle, but rather as an automatic ritual. I feel sure that very few non-Jewish parents could provide any real reason for the circumcision of their sons. . . ." He further states that "the operation has become a custom, an unthinking habit."

Doctor Atkinson then condemns his fellow-surgeons as being responsible for making circumcision "fashion-

able" and, as a consequence, he warns that this practice
"is very deplorable because it brings surgery into dis-
repute." [1]

Because a child "gets over it" is no argument in its
favor. Children get over pneumonia, infantile paralysis,
measles, scarlet fever, spinal meningitis, injuries sus-
tained in automobile and other accidents, but that is no
reason why they should be exposed to these dangerous
hazards.

Doctor Morris Fishbein, Editor in Chief of the
American Medical Journal, in discussing the subject in
his book, *Modern Home Medical Adviser,* states, "We
do not advocate that all boys and men be circumcised
. . ." [2] He then admonishes that "the boy baby should
be carefully examined to see if he needs circumcision.
If the foreskin can be quickly and easily retracted, *most
authorities think that circumcision should not be done.*
. . ." [3] (Italics mine)

I defy any reputable physician or surgeon to tell me
that he is able, on the eighth day of birth, to determine
whether or not the male infant should be circumcised!

However, many physicians give as an excuse for circumcision the assumption that there is generally in the
new-born male infant the presence of a normal phimosis—the medical term for the "adhesion" of the prepuce to the glans penis. While this is true, it is only a

[1] Atkinson, *Behind The Mask of Medicine,* pp. 181-183.
[2] P. 139.
[3] P. 83.

temporary condition and is usually corrected by the first erection during childhood, and hardly without notice by the child himself.

The presence of this so-called phimosis indicates that this "adhesion" has a definite purpose in protecting the glans penis until it begins its own development and is ready for the function intended for it. It is proof of the delicacy of the organ and Nature's attempt to protect it. The presence of this temporary adhesion of the prepuce in the infant male prompts me to ask: Has this phimosis in the male the same purpose as the hymen has in the female?

The presence of a complete phimosis which interferes with the child's urination is not pertinent to this study. A deformity of the glans penis is just as likely to occur as a deformity of the head, arms, legs, or other parts of the body. Then, and then only, should the surgeon's knife be used.

While ignorant man in the past brutally deflowered young girls because of the man's fear of being contaminated by the blood from the breaking of the hymen, this practice today has been discontinued. We now know that the purpose and function of the hymen is to protect the vagina until the first coitus.[4]

It would be just as idiotic to deflower all female infants at birth because, in later life some may develop a

---

[4] For more detailed analysis of this subject, see Lewis, *The Ten Commandments;* Briffault, *The Mothers;* Westermarck, *History of Human Marriage;* Crowley, *The Mystic Rose.*

tough hymen which the male on his wedding night is unable to penetrate, making an operation necessary, as it is to circumcise all male infants because in later life the phimosis of a few might require the surgeon's attention.

Doctor Atkinson takes full cognizance of this condition, and in his characteristically scientific analysis, makes the following very pertinent observation. His words of wisdom are too valuable not to quote at length.

"If a baby has a phimosis, a tight foreskin which cannot be retracted, circumcision is advocated on the grounds of cleanliness," but he hastens to add that "subpreputial ablutions are of no great importance in infancy, the necessity arises only as the child gets older. By that time, however, the normal processes of maturation will in the great majority of cases have converted what was a phimosis in babyhood into a normally retractile prepuce. It would seem to be the course of wisdom to await the workings of Nature, rather than presume that they will not occur. If they do not, it is time enough to take operative steps which still can be effective and need not necessarily be mutilating. The only phimosis in an infant which absolutely demands treatment is that which is so extreme that it interferes with urination. Such cases are not common. All others can safely be left alone in the expectation of normal maturation. We do not advocate the destruction of nailbeds on the fingers of all male infants lest dirt collect beneath the nails. Rather, we teach children the principles of cleanliness, and how and where to apply them. Yet the removal of nails would be just as logical as circumcision when the latter operation is performed on the usual excuse."

After an exhaustive analysis of the pros and cons of the subject, Doctor Atkinson concludes with these words: "To sum up the case, the weight of factual evidence is strongly against circumcision. . . . Aesthetically, it is undoubtedly bad—at best, a mutilation, at worst a tragedy." [5]

Could there be a more scathing condemnation of circumcision, from a medical point of view, than this damning indictment by Doctor Atkinson? Remember his words the next time someone tells you that the "medical profession" recommends circumcision.

The medical profession does nothing of the kind. It recommends circumcision only upon the advice of a competent physician when there exists a very definite reason for the operation. And those times are rare indeed, and still rarer in infants.

I cannot more appropriately conclude this chapter than by quoting the opinion of one of the foremost members of the American medical profession, Doctor Julius S. Weingart, Director, Department of Pathology, Iowa Lutheran Hospital, Des Moines, Iowa. In a letter to me dated July 21, 1948, he writes: "I am so thoroughly in accord with your contention that I must write at once to tell you so. As a routine procedure it

[5] *Loc. cit.,* pp. 177-183.

[circumcision] is merely the continuation of a most barbarous and savage practice." [1]

[1] As this book goes to press, I have been informed of a case involving the horrible mutilation of an infant following its circumcision by a Mohel.

From the very first day after he was circumcised and for the following *eight* months, the child cried continuously. The mother was driven almost to distraction, since the doctors who examined the child, found him normal in every respect. Her heart bled for her child and, finally, in desperation, she decided to visit her old family physician for advice. He, too, found the child perfectly normal. However, he noticed that the child's penis was not developing normally with the other parts of his body. A closer examination revealed that the circumcision was a frightfully bungled job. This condition was responsible for the child's being in continuous pain, resulting in his pitiful cries of agony. An operation by the physician was necessary to correct the mutilated condition left by the Mohel, and within a short time thereafter, the child ceased its crying.

The above facts were confirmed by the attending physician.

What intense suffering did this innocent child endure for eight long months! And for what? A mutilation following a useless operation by a brutal, ignorant and incompetent religionist!

Chapter VI

IS CIRCUMCISION A PREVENTIVE
OF VENEREAL DISEASES?

As STATED previously, when facts disprove the premise of a religious observance, specious arguments are resorted to as an excuse for its continuance. There is no accounting for the fantastic opinions formed from false arguments, especially when they are sought to justify the continuance of a superstitious practice. Superstition truly dies hard!

With circumcision exposed as a religious rite and having no value from the standpoint of hygiene, the arguments of the religious apologist shifted to the equally untenable premise that circumcision is a preventive of venereal diseases. It is nothing of the kind. Circumcision has no more value in preventing venereal diseases than it has in the field of hygiene. Reliance upon it as a protection against these diseases has only proved a dismal and tragic failure.

Doctor Atkinson, after studying the question of circumcision as a protection against venereal disease in relation to his own son, had this to say: "An operation is such a disturbing factor, and that of circumcision being what it is and where it is, perhaps more than most, I confess that I, in considering the advisability or otherwise of circumcision for my own infant son, should be very much more concerned with the implication of an operation than with the likelihood of his contracting gonorrhea or syphilis in twenty years' time. I should consider it possible, even perhaps hope it probable, that in the course of those years I might be able to guide him towards a way of life and thought more surely preventive of those diseases than circumcision. It has always seemed to me a very queer argument." [1]

In a discussion regarding circumcision as a disease preventive, a prominent Health Officer of one of our larger cities stated most emphatically that it was utterly without value. To support this conviction, he related the following experience:

A man came to him to be circumcised. After a very careful examination, he told his patient that he found no condition of his male organ that would justify such an operation. The doctor asked why he wanted to be circumcised. He told the doctor that he was of the belief that if he were circumcised it would protect him against contracting a venereal disease. The doctor told him that such an opinion was a popular misconception and was entirely false. He stated that circumcision is not a preventive of venereal disease, and that as a physician devoting his energies to public health,

[1] *Loc. cit.,* pp. 180, 181.

he had seen too many cases in which circumcised men were its victims, and that if the patient should come in contact with a woman who had a venereal disease, he would in all probability be infected, whether circumcised or not.

The man thanked the doctor for enlightening him upon the subject but left the office with a puzzled expression upon his face. He was trying to decide whether he should continue his promiscuous sexual conduct as in the past, since the danger of disease was so menacing.

The *Jewish Encyclopedia* has taken cognizance of this false argument that circumcision is a preventive of venereal diseases and makes this pertinent comparison which should settle for all time the falsity of this defense. It states: "The glans of the circumcised, besides being uncovered, presents another change to which considerable importance has been attached. The covering of the glans, which before had the character of a mucous membrane, on being exposed assumed the properties of true skin, which is less vulnerable and on theoretical grounds alone leads to the inference that it is less liable to syphilitic infection," but the writer concludes his observation with these emphatic words: he *"has observed too many cases of primary syphilis in the circumcised to warrant the assumption that circumcision offers any very decided immunity."* [2] (Italics mine.)

[2] *Jewish Encyclopedia,* Vol. 4, p. 101.

Chapter VII

IS CIRCUMCISION A PREVENTIVE
OF CANCER?

SOME TIME AGO, I had occasion to rebuke a writer in a nationally circulated magazine, who had written an article on circumcision, in which she stated among other erroneous opinions, that it was a preventive of cancer.

The number of cases of cancer of the glans penis is so small compared to its attack upon other parts of the body, that circumcision for that reason is not only wholly unjustified, but beneath the dignity of an educated person's consideration.

By what perverted method of reasoning is such an operation justified when there are more deaths as a result of circumcision than there are of cancer of the prepuce?

If the prepuce, as with other parts of the body, is subject to cancer, why not wait until the disease makes its appearance, *then* apply the surgeon's knife? Why circumcise over a million children in order to prevent cancer from attacking only *one* of them? Yes, that is the percentage!

Let me quote Doctor Atkinson on this important phase of the subject: ". . . cancer of the penis never occurs in the circumcised. For that matter, it occurs very rarely in the uncircumcised, either. It is a far cry from infancy to venereal disease, it is a much farther cry to that rare disease, penile cancer, and does not seem to have any serious bearing on the point at issue." [1]

The most eloquent testimony that can be used in exposing the false arguments in favor of circumcision as a preventive of cancer is the mere recital of the prosaic figures which are released in the statistical report of the Cancer Record Registry, Division of Cancer and Other Chronic Diseases, Connecticut State Department of Health.

From these statistics, we find that cancer of the "glans and foreskin of the penis" occurs on 0.2 per 100,000, while cancer of the "Testis, epididymis, Spermatic Cord," occurs 2.0 per 100,000, or *ten times* more than that of the Glans and Foreskin of Penis; while cancer of the "Prostate, Seminal Vesicles and Adnexae" occurs 20.4 per 100,000, or more than *100 times* more than that of the "Glans and Foreskin of Penis."

Therefore, by the same process of reasoning based upon these facts, all male children should either be castrated or have all their sexual organs removed at birth, since there exists a far greater likelihood of cancer in that area of the body than in the prepuce and glans penis!

These statistics are even more devastating when considered in relation to the prevalence of cancer of the

[1] *Loc. cit.*, p. 181.

female breast. This same authority reports that cancer of the breast occurs in females 13.8 per 100,000, which is more than *50 times* the frequency with which cancer attacks the glans and foreskin of the penis.[2]

Again, by the same process of reasoning, all adolescent females should have their breasts removed in order to avoid cancer of that area.

How ridiculous becomes the advocacy of circumcision as a preventive of cancer, in the face of this scientific searchlight upon this important matter.

[2] The nomenclature used is the nomenclature of diagnosis of the Memorial Hospital for the Treatment of Cancer and Allied Diseases, New York City.

Chapter VIII

THE DANGERS AND FATAL CONSEQUENCES OF CIRCUMCISION

My Cousin's Child

WHEN I was informed that a cousin of mine had given birth to a boy, I called to offer my congratulations. It was indeed a happy event, because she had been married for quite some time and had despaired of ever having a child. I was told that, while the mother was doing well, the child was in a delicate condition that required the most careful medical supervision in order that it might survive.

I immediately communicated with my cousin's mother to urge that they do not circumcise the child.

Such a thought had never occurred to them, as they believed that circumcision was performed upon all male children as part of their natural existence. I pleaded with them. I told them that circumcision had nothing whatever to do with health and hygiene, and that it was but a ritual performance which should have been abolished centuries ago with many other old primitive and obsolete customs and superstitions.

My pleadings were of no avail.

I then urged that if they were determined to circumcise the child, that they put it off to a future date when he would be better able to stand such an ordeal. My pleadings, again, were in vain. They not only ignored my suggestion but even ignored me as a manifestation of their resentment for my having made such a blasphemous proposal.

And so, on the eighth day of the infant's birth, as provided by the Biblical edict, the child was circumcised. Within one month he was dead!

MY NIECE'S SECOND CHILD

When I was notified by my sister that her daughter had given birth to a second child, this time a boy, I could detect in her voice the joy she was experiencing. I nevertheless noticed a slight concern in her expression. Upon further inquiry, I was told that the child had been born prematurely and weighed little more than four pounds. I most strongly suggested to her that the child be permitted to grow up with all the flesh with which Nature had endowed it, and stressed the fact that it was dangerous to circumcise a child weighing so little, particularly since he had been born prematurely. My sister informed her daughter of my advice, and she and her husband talked the matter over.

The pressure from the paternal grandparents was too strong to avoid circumcising him, but upon consulting their physician, he informed them that he would not allow the child, in its delicate state, to be circumcised, and insisted that it weigh at least eight pounds before undergoing such an operation.

When the child was two months old, the physician himself performed the operation. The postponement of nearly seven weeks, brought about by my objections, probably saved the child's life but it did not prevent its mutilation.

A MENOPAUSE BABY

This story was told to me by a dear personal friend, who is a poet, an author, and one of the prominent business men in the United States. One of his old and trusted employees, a shipping clerk, came to him one day, with an expression of joy on his face, and told him that after having been married for nearly twenty years, his wife was going to have a baby! My friend wished him the best of luck and gave him a full measure of help and cooperation.

The baby came. It was a boy. It was healthy and normal in every respect. A perfect specimen of a new-born infant. The physician who attended the delivery of the child was a Catholic, as were the parents. The doctor suggested that the child be circumcised, and the proud, happy parents, anxious to do all in their power for the child, consented.

After the operation, the child fell asleep and the mother put it tenderly into its crib. A few hours later, beaming with mother love, she looked at her child to see how he was getting along. She found the sheet blood-soaked and the baby dead! It had bled to death!

Several days later, the father came into the office of my friend in a state of great emotional stress, and told him what had happened. He was so unnerved and so burning with indignation, particularly since he knew that he and his wife would never have another child, that he asked his employer to prevent him from carrying out his determination to kill the doctor who had been responsible for the death of his infant son.

Only those who have lost their first and only child are able to understand the grief that this man suffered.

A Physician's Experience

When I asked a physician friend of mine to send me some details of his experience with circumcision, he wrote that he had personal knowledge of fatal results in two cases.

One was that of a woman who had given birth and who showed signs of being a hemophiliac, but whose husband insisted that the child be circumcised. My friend argued, as a physician, against it. Despite his protests, however, the child was circumcised. The results he predicted followed, and, he writes, "in spite of repeated transfusions and other treatments to check the bleeding, it bled to death."

In the other case, he writes, "there was a definite history of hemophilia in the family," and so, when the child was born, he opposed its being circumcised. The father was an orthodox believer in Judaism who insisted that the rite be performed according to the Hebrew ritual. "I pleaded with him to forego circumcision in his son," states the physician, and then records that the father said, "The Lord will protect the child. I would rather see the boy dead than live uncircumcised." The father's wish was granted. The physician reports that "the child died within fifteen minutes after the ceremony. . . ."

Whether or not this tragic result shook the faith of this orthodox believer in the Lord, I made no further inquiry.

There are no medical statistics available as to how many children have died as a result of circumcision. In the English medical journal *Lancet* for October 1, 1870, there is reported two deaths from circumcision: one five days and the other twenty-five days after the operation. In the same periodical of December 5, 1874, there is reported by a Dr. Kohn six deaths resulting from circumcision, one being his own child.[1]

A Doctor's Dilemma

I was recently told of a case where a child was circumcised on the eighth day of its birth, in accordance with the Biblical injunction. The circumcision was performed by a Mohel. Immediately after the operation, the child suffered a hemorrhage which became so serious that the family physician was called in immediately.

The physician found the child in such a critical condition that he sent for a blood specialist. The specialist was so alarmed at the condition of the child that he

[1] Quoted from *The Barbarity of Circumcision,* by Dr. Herbert Snow.

immediately brought in two other blood specialists for consultation. The physicians did everything within their knowledge and power to stop the bleeding, without results, and they gave the child up as a hopeless case. He seemed doomed to an inevitable death. However, just before leaving, one of the doctors squeezed the organ and the bleeding ceased, evidently the pressure causing a cessation of bleeding. The other remedies they resorted to may also have been responsible for saving its life.

This case is an instance that circumcision becomes a medical problem only after the child has been circumcised. If it had not been for expert medical attention, the child would have surely died.

That such tragedies have happened in the past is verified by references in the Jewish Encyclopedia regarding the circumcision of children of feeble constitution.

A Friend's Child

A friend writes me that the climax of his troubled life came after listening to others regarding the circumcising of his child. He permitted circumcision when the child was seven years old and he died as a result of the operation!

Vitamin K

We now know why fatal results sometimes follow the circumcising of a child on the eighth day after its birth, as well as why some children bleed to death after this operation. It is because the child is physically unable to stand the severity of this surgical operation, during the first few days of its life.

Science is responsible for this life-saving knowledge. Doctor Karl Lansteiner's researches into the composition of human blood and the remarkable discoveries which have followed his findings are of incalculable value to the human race.

As a result of the foundation of knowledge that he laid down concerning the composition and the variations of the human blood, we have since discovered that the reason for the coagulating quality of blood is the presence of what is now known as *Vitamin K*. This vitamin, responsible for the coagulation of the blood, does not form in the body until the *tenth* day after birth, and then only in a normal, healthy child.

Science has also discovered that the child inherits a sufficient quantity of prothrombin, a blood-coagulating quality, from its mother to start it on its growth. This *decreases* during the first few days of life, until the child's own body begins to develop this vitally important quality. Circumcision interferes with this process in the body.

This great discovery has been responsible, by verifiable statistics, for saving at least three percent of the recent number of new-born children. This has been accomplished because physicians now take no chances on this deficiency being present in a new-born infant. They make sure that the pregnant woman possesses a sufficient amount of prothrombin in her blood by a scientific test, and, if deficient, she is given a diet rich in *Vitamin K*.

We now know that hemophilia, an hereditary blood disease, is transmitted only through a mother to her son, and is a dominant inherited characteristic.

Also, as a precautionary measure, if the child is a likely victim of hemorrhage, a sufficient quantity of *Vitamin K* is injected into the new-born infant. The attending physician should be fully acquainted with the family history in this matter, and use every precautionary measure to save the child.

Hebrew ecclesiastics in modern times, cognizant of the number of deaths which have resulted from circumcision but wholly unacquainted and unfamiliar with the scientific reasons, exempted certain children from being subjected to this Biblical rite. The ecclesiastical rule is that if *two* children of the same family have *died* as a result of circumcision, the circumcision of the third child must be postponed.

Hebrew ecclesiastics also exempt a child suffering from a fever as well as those suffering from infections such as sore eyes and similar illnesses. These children, who suffer from these afflictions, must, however, when cured, be subjected to the circumcision rite.[2]

If circumcision was truly a token of the covenant betwixt a person and his god, then there would be no

[2] Wm. Rosenau, *Jewish Ceremonial Institution and Customs,* Bloch Publishing Co., N. Y., 1929. Also, *Laws and Customs of Israel,* translated by Gerald Friedlander, Shapiro, Vallentine & Co., London, 1929; also, *Jewish Encyclopedia,* "Circumcision," Vol. 4, pp. 92 to 102.

deaths as a result of it; on the contrary, it should prove the preserver, not the destroyer, of life.

But because this Biblical injunction is not a *token* but purely a superstitious rite, no child is exempt from its dangers, despite the presence of pious attendants, supposed to make it doubly holy, and fervent prayers for blessings of the Bible Deity.

THE MOVING FINGER

If your child should be subjected to this primitive superstitious rite of blood atonement and fatal results should follow, all the tears and heartaches of the world will not bring your son back to life.

Because, the Bible Deity to the contrary notwithstanding, when,

> "The moving finger writes; and, having writ,
>   Moves on: nor all your Piety nor Wit
>   Shall lure it back to cancel half a Line,
>   Nor all your Tears wash out a Word of it."

MY GRANDSON

When my daughter's child was about to be born, I told her that if it were a boy, I would be very much opposed to his being circumcised. Knowing my feelings in the matter, she naturally was inclined to obey my wishes.

However, as the time approached for the birth of the child, she discussed the matter with her obstetrician. He told her that if the child were a boy, he would urge

that it be circumcised. My daughter's confidence in her
physician began to create doubts in her mind as to the
correctness of my views. A pregnant woman is very
susceptible to the authority of her doctor.

The question of whether to circumcise or not was an
ever-recurrent topic of family discussion. One evening
at dinner, when we began to discuss the matter, I noticed a concerned expression in her eyes.

She had made a routine visit to her doctor on this
particular day, and during the course of his examination, he asked her whether she had made up her mind
concerning the circumcising of the child in the event
it was a boy.

She replied that she had discussed the matter again
with me; that my views and opinions against it were
more pronounced than ever. In order to dispel all
doubts in the mind of my daughter, her physician told
her that a certain well-known non-sectarian hospital in
New York considered circumcision so important that
every male child, whether Christian or Jewish, born
in that hospital was, as a matter of regular procedure,
obliged to be circumcised. This was certainly a convin-
cing argument to my daughter, and it produced a series
of confused doubts in her mind; she was deeply concerned about the matter and was in a dilemma as to
what to do. She knew of the sincerity of my conviction
and yet she respected highly the medical knowledge of
her physician.

Here was a serious situation. I did not want to shake
her confidence in her doctor at this late date, as the
child was expected within two or three months; how-

ever, I could not let such a statement go unchallenged. I told her very frankly that I did not believe the physician's statement and that I did not think any hospital would be guilty of such a presumptuous order.

I then said that there was only one way to determine the truth of the physician's statement, and that was to call the hospital on the telephone for verification.

My daughter reluctantly agreed to this test. I made the call and spoke to the manager. I asked whether it was true that all male children born in that hospital had to be circumcised, and the emphatic reply was that such a statement was too ridiculous to believe; and that a male child was circumcised in that hospital only upon the written request of its parents.

Upon hearing the conversation and the repudiation of her physician's statement, my daughter was visibly affected. I tried to console her by saying that I still considered her physician a good one, and that she should not make any change to another at that time. But I had to condemn him, nevertheless, for his method of trying to convince her. She told him what I had done and to his credit he never mentioned the subject again.

The result of my persuasion was soon evident. The child was born five weeks prematurely and the physician performed his task capably and well, saving both my daughter and her child. The baby weighed a little over four pounds at birth.

However, her ordeal in this matter was not at an end. Her regular family physician visited her at the hospital, and, ignoring completely her weakened physical

condition resulting from the severity of her confinement, annoyed her persistently to have the child circumcised. I arrived at the hospital shortly after the
doctor had left, and noticing her in an agitated condition, asked her what was the matter. She reluctantly
related the cause of her emotionally upset condition.

I told her not to worry, that if this doctor should
ever mention the subject to her again, I would inflict
upon him a physical chastisement that he would long
remember, and that it would make him hesitate again
to ever torment a mother by insisting that her child be
so cruelly mutilated.

And now for the important result of my persistence.
The child was not doing well, and he was certainly a
pitiful sight. Despite the fact that he was kept in a
"hot bed" and given the best of care the hospital was
capable of rendering, the pediatrician urged, as a precautionary measure, and because of the shortage of hospital nurses, that the child be taken home as quickly as
possible and be given the strictest attention by a special
nurse.

Fortunately, the pediatrician was opposed to circumcision, as he was fully acquainted with the results of
trauma upon children following operations before they
are a year old. These shocks upon the infant's tender,
susceptible and impressionable brain, often leave last-
ing and irremedial injuries.

An excellent nurse, strict supervision, and the best
of care have been responsible for the growth and development of a sound and healthy boy.

I am confident that if this child had been circumcised

in the regular way, and at the prescribed time after its birth, he would have died. Being delicate, prematurely born, and weighing little more than four pounds, and my daughter herself being a "bleeder," he would have been unable to withstand the shock and loss of precious blood so necessary for the preservation of his life.

And so I say to my grandson,

"If life holds any pleasures, give a thought, now and then, to your grandpa for having preserved it for you."

Chapter IX

THE PSYCHOLOGICAL DANGERS
OF CIRCUMCISION

THE EVILS and dangers of circumcision are not only in the mutilation of an important organ of the body and the unnecessary pain inflicted upon the infant, but the hidden and not easily detected injuries are in many instances far more serious and menacing than those more readily discernible. These are the injuries resulting from the shock to the nervous system.

If you knew the severity of the operation involved in circumcision, the pain and distress it causes, perhaps you would better understand the seriousness of the psychological effect of such an impact upon the tender brain of a new-born infant.

Doctor Atkinson condemns circumcision not only from the medical and surgical points of view, but also because of this dangerous psychological effect upon the child.

I quote the poignant, yet eloquent words of this eminent physician: "Speaking solely of circumcision in the infant and child, perhaps the most important effect, as it is the least considered, is the psychological. But, you may say, what psychological effect can there possibly be in an infant of eight days, or even of eight weeks? More, perhaps, than we think. . . .

"In point of fact, according to the rules, the new-born infant should be a very suitable subject for psychological injury. . . . What greater transition could there be than from the womb to the world. . . .

"If, under those circumstances, long before you had found feet or bearings in this strange new world into which you had so suddenly been precipitated, there fell upon you a Man with a Knife who mutilated you and changed one of the few pleasures (the excretory functions are alleged to be very pleasurable to a child) into burning pain, would you not feel some resentment? Because not all babies show psychological trauma in this way is not evidence that the ones that do not show it do not feel it. . . . In the weeks immediately after the operation, there is seen only too often acute distress in both mother and child, distress so acute that it cannot help recurring to the mind whenever circumcision is mooted. . . . Then there is the question of anaesthesia. The older child is given an anaesthetic, the infant commonly is not. . . . Therefore one would urge that in all cases an anaesthetic should be given. But anaesthetics are not without their dangers, and have special dangers to young organisms. *The dealth of a healthy baby under anaesthesia for an operation of doubtful propriety is a thing not to be contemplated. . . ."* (Italics mine) [1]

[1] *Behind the Mask of Medicine,* pp. 178 to 179.

Today medical science knows that trauma—shock—leaves its effect upon the nervous system.

In many instances, these negative reactions to shock manifest themselves in symptoms with which the physician is unable to cope, primarily because he cannot trace the ailment to the particular shock that caused it. These shocks are generally the ones experienced during early childhood. Medical science is cognizant of this psychological fact and now warns both parent and physician to avoid, as much as possible, any act that might leave an indelibly negative impression upon the mind of the child. It is urged that the same caution be exercised in this respect that is now used toward contagious diseases.

The child has come into a world of a thousand bewildering torments. Remember your own anxiety when beset with a serious illness, your body burning with fever and your mind beset with fear, then reflect for a moment upon a child's reaction in such a dilemma.

Remember, when in dealing with him under like circumstances, his anxiety is far deeper, his suffering more intense, and he is additionally handicapped by the fact that he is unable to tell you of the intensity of the pain he suffers or what part of the body is affected.

The task of raising a child who is normal in every respect is difficult enough without complicating this endeavor by unnecessary obstacles.

Parents little realize that many of the acts which they condemn in their children, and for which they often administer corporal punishment as a corrective, are often due to their own ignorant and thoughtless conduct.

How many children have cried in protest against threatened punishment by cruel parents, who have whipped them for acts from which they were unable to restrain themselves? How many have pitifully cried, in defense, "I tried not to do it," "I didn't want to do it?"

How do we know that this inability of a child to control his "will" is not the result of some form of shock which undermined his mentality and diminished his ability to control his acts?

It is definitely established that shock affects adversely the physical system. How much more so the mind?

To all parents, may I interpose this advice:

Don't beat your child.

Don't frighten your child.

Don't abuse your child.

If he provokes you by his conduct, remember that he is struggling to adjust himself in a world not of his making nor to his liking.

It is YOU who should control your impulses, and not give vent to your irritation by punishing your child.

The child's task in adjusting himself is difficult enough as it is. He is bewildered far beyond his comprehension and he hasn't the strength mentally nor physically to control or direct his acts.

I am aware that bringing up a child is a difficult undertaking, and I know how provoking he can be at times; but try to bear in mind that understanding, sympathy and indulgence are the obligations of the parents. They should not be shirked, and must not be abused.

However, what is past is done.

If the human race is to continue to exist, let us strive to develop a race of free and courageous men and women. This cannot be done by punishing others for our mistakes. The least we can do is to permit our children to grow and develop in mind and body as Nature intended, and to avoid, through ignorance or callous brutality, mutilating their bodies and crippling their minds with fears and inhibitions.

Medical science is already beginning to trace certain permanent ailments in the adult to shocks experienced in childhood. These shocks have been characterized as "delayed action mines." In fact, this is the very principle upon which psychosomatic medicine is based.

One of the foremost authorities in this field of modern medicine is Doctor Flanders Dunbar of Columbia College of Medicine. In her recent book she records the results of her investigations and makes these significant statements:

"Disaster to the exploring childish mind may not come with an immediate crash. It is far more likely to be unnoticed—or at least disregarded—at the time. But the harvest of childhood's experiences may be reaped years later and turn out to be the fundamental or contributing cause of an illness which has no surface connection with the patient's past.

"These are the delayed-action mines of childhood, planted either in the shock of some single incident or in the steady friction of a conflict between mind and environment. Once these mines have been planted, they may become covered over with a thick, hard crust of oblivion, but they never cease to be dangerous unless the fuses can be drawn." [2]

In circumcision, the "fuses" cannot be drawn. They have already become so deeply imbedded in the unconscious mind of the child, "covered over with the thick hard crust of oblivion," that no remedial measures can possibly eradicate them.

They must "explode." And into what hidden areas these explosions may penetrate no one knows, but the very best that may be hoped for is to try to arrest them and to minimize their effect. Even this endeavor rarely meets with success.

The analysis of the individual cases which brought out these startling facts is worthy of very serious consideration.

Doctor Dunbar found that "an unusually large proportion [of the patients] had neurotic traits in childhood. These expressed themselves for some of the patients in the form of walking or talking in their sleep, in others as persistent lying, stealing and truancy. Later these tendencies disappeared, apparently replaced by the accident habit." [3]

Many of the diseases of childhood can now be traced to some form of shock in infancy, and while there are some children's diseases which apparently cannot be avoided, it has been fairly well established that their

[2] *Mind and Body*, p. 17.
[3] *Ibid.*, p. 101.

severity is increased where the child's resistance to shock is diminished.

Even allergies, skin diseases, stammering and stuttering are often the results of shock. Here is what Doctor Dunbar has to say about one phase of "delayed action mine explosions:"

"One of the delayed-action mines of childhood explodes, appropriately enough, on the surface. The explosion takes the form of the common skin diseases, and the fuse is usually shorter than that of most other such mines. Eczema and its medical relations generally make their appearance while the victim is still young." [4]

Medical science, fortunately, is now taking cognizance of this relationship. Here is an instance: Rheumatic fever in childhood is on the increase. It is a dangerous and terrifying disease in itself. But it also leads to a still more fatal ailment—heart disease.

It is now established that "under ordinary circumstances, from 50 to 75 percent of children with rheumatic fever may be expected to contract heart disease." [5]

And heart disease causes one-third of the deaths today. The significant relationship between these two diseases is shown by this pertinent fact: that rheumatic fever which attacks with such crippling devastation children between the ages of five and fifteen is the cause of nearly forty per cent of heart fatalities in adult life. [6]

Because of the growing prevalence of circumcision,

[4] *Ibid.*, p. 190.
[5] *Hygeia*, Dec., 1947.
[6] *Ibid.*

how many children who now suffer from this terrible affliction can trace its origin to the impact of the shock received from this unnecessary and frightfully painful operation!

It is well known to the medical profession that innumerable afflictions are directly traceable to shock. How often have physicians been called in to treat persons who, suddenly confronted with shocking news, are in a state of mental or physical collapse.

And more cases than the public is aware of never recover. Our insane asylums are mute testimony of these tragedies. I know of two cases personally where unexpected shock resulted in physical afflictions.

A mother had expected her daughter home from the hospital for the mentally sick, believing her to be cured. She was anxiously awaiting her arrival, when the telephone rang. In a happy, expectant state, she answered the telephone, and was informed by the hospital attendants that her daughter had just hanged herself!

As if struck by a bolt of lightning, the mother stood motionless and impassive as if paralyzed. She finally collapsed. Within one week her body was covered with sores; her face was a horrible mass of pus-broken skin. Medical treatment was of no avail. It took three months for her body to function normally after this shock. Shortly afterwards, the sores disappeared. The deep, terrifying scars upon her mind, however, remained. When they may break out in another form of malady, no one knows.

In relating these instances, remember we are dealing

with adults. The reaction in infants is a thousand times more intense.

Here is the other case: A wife, after many years of marriage, and presumably devoted to her husband who had become successful and had attained a high social standing, was suddenly discovered to have been guilty of gross marital indiscretions during all the years of her marriage. When she was confronted with her flagrant misconduct, which she thought would never be discovered, and realizing the disgrace that would follow the public revelation of her guilty conduct, the shock of exposure brought about such a reaction that within a few days, large, unsightly sores began to appear over her body. Her legs and arms were covered. Blotches appeared on her face. She presented a horrible and distressing sight. When she went out, in order to avoid the gaze of the curious, she wore dark-colored glasses, heavy black stockings to cover the sores on her legs, and long black gloves to hide the unsightly appearance of her arms.

Added to her anxiety was the fear that she had contracted syphilis, and she had several Wasserman tests made.

Dermatologists and blood specialists were unable to help her. Her affliction was medically diagnosed as "shock." More than a year elapsed before the sores disappeared, and the skin assumed its normal appearance.

If an adult can suffer such a reaction to shock, what terrifying emotions are indelibly seared into the mind of a helpless infant? Who knows how permanent the injury and how long-lasting the shock!

Does anyone think for a moment that a new-born babe, suddenly being pounced upon by a *Man with a Knife,* his flesh cut and torn in the tenderest part of his body, suffers no psychological reaction to this shocking brutality?

And now for proof that the shock of circumcision is the cause of some of these "delayed action mines," which so adversely affect the child's nervous system and hamper its normal development.

Doctor David M. Levy, one of the greatest living child psychiatrists, warns his fellow-physicians against the dangers of operation upon children of tender ages, particularly before the age of two years. Doctor Levy made a very exhaustive study of the results of trauma to the nervous system of the child resulting from such operations.

His findings, for the guidance of his fellow-physicians, appeared in the *American Journal of Diseases of Children,* and are entitled, "Psychic Trauma of Operations in Children." [7] His facts are highly significant to this study.

Doctor Levy states that, "impressed by the number of cases in which fears, anxieties and other symptoms closely followed an operative procedure, I reviewed my records for some years past in order to determine how frequently such difficulties arose."

In undertaking this study and making these observa-

[7] Vol. 69, Jan., 1945, pp. 7 to 25.

tions, Doctor Levy pursued new avenues in the field of medical science, and the results of his investigation produced invaluable knowledge in revealing the post-operative results of shock in the infant.

He found that "a frightening experience of any kind presumably has an effect inversely proportional to the child's mastery of the situation." Doctor Levy discovered that the younger the child, the keener was its response to pain and that, "for them, the operative experience is more acute in every phase . . . and is a raw and brutal experience. . . ."

He traced, as the direct result of shock, one of the most terrifying experiences of childhood—night terrors, which he describes as "a break-through of fear during sleep." The length of time it takes for these nightmares to "wear off" depends upon the intensity of the shock resulting from the operation or some similar frightening experience.

These shocks may never wear off in childhood and may manifest themselves in adult life by anti-social conduct.

How do we know how many become unadjusted to life's mores, how many become mental misfits, how many go into the insane asylum? Still worse, how many, unconsciously unable to account for their destructive impulses, become criminals seeking vengeance upon society for their inability to adjust themselves in the competitive scheme of life?

Doctor Levy records a case involving the circumcision of a boy of six years and seven months. He speaks of the struggle of the patient with his father and the anaesthetist before they overpowered him. "The father," Doctor Levy says, "felt 'sick about it for a week' because the whole experience was 'so brutal.'"

After the operation, the boy's "previous temper developed into destructive rages . . . [he] played numerous killing games . . . developed claustrophobia . . . destructive behavior and occasional suicidal impulses continued. . . ."

Doctor Levy records another case of a boy of four years of age. Immediately after circumcision, the child developed suicidal impulses, "and his play was in the form of destroying things, cutting people up and burning them. His type of play had to do with a fear of castration immediately following a meatotomy. It dealt directly with the focus of anxiety."

In still another case, a boy had been brought to him at the age of three years and seven months. He suffered from "temper tantrums, fears, restless behavior and night terrors." These symptoms began immediately after the boy had been circumcised at the age of one year.

Only one who has seen a child in the grip of a nightmare can realize what tortures and torments he experiences. They are almost too frightening for description. Only after an almost interminable period of screaming and despairing helplessness, which no comforting can assuage, does the child fall asleep from sheer exhaustion.

I had a younger brother who suffered from this

affliction. To the best of my memory he was possibly two or three years old. I was four years his senior. We slept in the same bed together. Quite frequently, I now recall, after reading Doctor Levy's article, my brother would suddenly awake in the middle of the night and begin to scream in a most agonizing manner. Before I could collect my own senses to call for help, his screams would awaken my mother who would come rushing into the room to soothe him.

I was informed by a mother that shortly after her child had been circumcised at the age of three years, he began to walk in his sleep, and this persisted for quite some time. The anxiety of the parents was that during his somnambulistic adventuring, the child would wander off with the imminent danger of injuring himself.

Another parent told me of the excessive bed-wetting which followed her son's circumcision.

Now, what about the other diseases of childhood which are too numerous to mention?

Since preventive medicine is just as important as curative medicine—particularly so, since the younger the child, the more frequently sickness strikes—why not give serious consideration to circumcision as a contributing cause of these ailments?

And, in addition, remember the grim fact that the largest percentage of infant mortality occurs before they are a year old.[8]

Are not the "ills that flesh is heir to" sufficient to

[8] *Facts About Child Health,* Federal Security Agency, Washington, D. C., 1946.

plague and torment us without adding more of our own making?

At least, let this be our attitude towards helpless infants. Give them the best opportunity to meet the impact of life's struggles. Don't *you* be guilty of acts which will hinder *your* child from developing into a normal, happy, human being.

Chapter X

THE OPERATION

IT IS the ignorance prevalent concerning the details involved in a circumcision operation that makes its practice so tragic. If people knew the facts, it would not only be abolished, but a penalty of punishment would be imposed upon those who were guilty of perpetrating it.

How many know the details involved in the circumcision operation?

How many know the pain and agony it causes?

How many know the potential dangers that are present?

How many know the permanent injuries that have followed it?

How many know the number of deaths that it has caused?

The general conception is that circumcision is but a simple act and that almost anyone can do it, and that it should be done and over with, as a matter of course, and the sooner the better.

It is also the general conception that the circumciser, whether he be Mohel, Rabbi or physician, merely takes a pair of scissors and cuts off the hanging prepuce as he would cut off a hanging nail.

What a terrifying difference between this false conception and the truth!

In order that there may be no misunderstanding about the details of the operation, I have taken the method used from the text as described by the *Jewish Encyclopedia,* lest I be charged with bias in presenting the details of it in this book.

The mere recital of the details involved in the operation is sufficient to condemn it.[1]

Read carefully the description of the steps taken and the caution advised in the performance of the operation, in order to properly comprehend what actually takes place when a child is circumcised:

"To perform the operation and to avoid any danger that may be connected with it, an acquaintance with the anatomy of the tissues involved is necessary. The organ terminates in a conical fleshy substance called the glans. The skin covering the organ is prolonged forward in a loose fold, which covers the glans and is supplied with an inner lining of the character of a mucous membrane, which, being retracted, also forms a covering of the glans proper. The prolonged portion of skin with its lining is termed the prepuce or foreskin. The prepuce has no large blood-vessels; and therefore circumcision is not attended by any dangerous hemorrhage, except when the *glans is injured by unskilful handling* of the knife, or in very exceptional cases where there exists an abnormal tendency to bleeding."

[1] Vol. IV, pp. 98 to 101. (All italics mine.)

The importance of medical knowledge of the tendency of hemophilia in the family was discussed in a previous chapter, as well as the importance of a sufficient amount of prothrombin in the blood before such an operation takes place.

That the Mohel or Rabbi is wholly without such knowledge is too obvious for comment, nor has he any "acquaintance with the anatomy of the tissues involved." There are no authorized schools in the United States under the supervision of either the medical profession or the state commissioners of education, where such knowledge is taught to equip them as circumcisers.

> "Circumcision varies considerably as practiced by the Jews and by the Mohammedans. Among the Jews it means not only the excision of the outer part of the prepuce, but also a slitting of its inner lining to facilitate the total uncovering of the glans. The Mohammedans pursue the simple method of cutting off the integumental portion of the foreskin, so that almost all of the inner layer remains, and the glans continues covered."

While the above description should be sufficient to convey what is actually done when the child is circumcised, I do not believe that mere words are sufficient to impart the painful reaction that comes from not only cutting off the outer skin of the prepuce, but of "the slitting of the inner lining" so as "to facilitate the total uncovering of the glans." This might be compared with the membrane which connects the tongue to the floor of the mouth. Imagine, if you can, slitting that part of the tongue from the lower part of the mouth, and you have an idea of what takes place in slitting the prepuce from the frenum of the glans to enable one to push back the remaining skin in order to completely expose the head of the penis. And again the healing of a cut in the mouth is immeasurably quicker than that of the genital organs.

> "The operation up to very recent times was exclusively performed by laymen, to whom the act had been taught by others who, by experience, had acquired the necessary knowledge and skill. The tests of a good operator, or "mohel" [circumciser], were that he should perform his work quickly, safely as to its immediate effect, and successfully as to the condition which the parts would permanently assume. As a rule, the majority of these operators developed great dexterity; and *accidents* were remarkably rare."

How many innocent children died while these "operators developed great dexterity" no one will ever know. The number of "accidents" are not recorded. *They have been buried.* The law *as yet* does not require that these operations be made a matter of public record. But it should, and it will, I hope, very soon. *Because if there was ever an instance of practicing medicine without a license, it is when one who is not a physician circumcises a child.*

If the Department of Health does not possess the power at the present time to impose such a regulation, then it should seek this authority, without delay, from the State Legislature.

And if any physician either recommends or performs a circumcision operation, unjustified by medical necessity, but solely for the purpose of a ritual compliance, he should be considered guilty of malpractice and severely punished.

> "In case the glans was not sufficiently exposed after the healing process was completed, much anxiety was occasioned; for in some exceptional instances *a second operation* was resorted to."

If ever proof of the incompetence of the religious circumciser is conclusive, it is the bungling of a circumcision, thus requiring a second operation. Is more evidence needed to prove his utter lack of medical knowledge?

The religious circumciser, with a knife in his hand, is ready, if necessary, to destroy a life in the performance of this ritual as "a fulfillment of the covenant of the Lord." And that is called an act of "Health and Hygiene."

> "The operation consists of three parts: 'milah,' 'peri'ah,' and 'mezizah':
>
> "Milah: The Child having been placed upon a pillow resting upon the lap of the godfather or 'sandek' (he who is honored by being assigned to hold the child), the mohel exposes the parts by removal of garments, etc., and instructs the sandek how to hold the child's legs. The mohel then grasps the prepuce between the thumb and index-finger of his left hand, exerting sufficient traction to draw it from the glans, and places the shield (see Fig. 1) in position just before the glans. He now takes his knife and with one sweep excises the foreskin. This completes the first act. The knife (see Fig. 3) most commonly used is double-edged, although one like those ordinarily used by surgeons is also often employed."

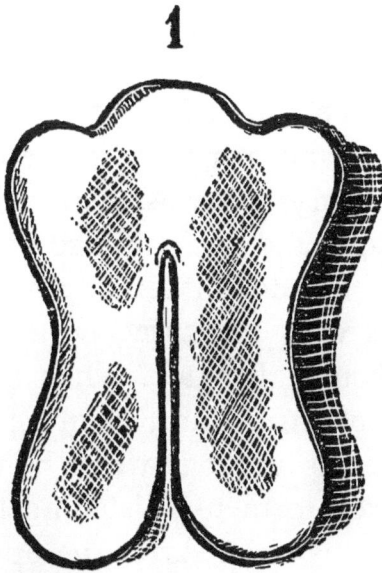

INSTRUMENTS USED IN CIRCUMCISION

It is almost impossible to believe that parents who love their children could stand by and see them so unmercifully tortured for a religious purpose. Can religion so stultify the brain that it even makes us callous to the cries of our loved ones when being so outrageously assaulted?

One mother writes that her son was circumcised upon the advice of her physician, and adds,

"When my son was circumcised at the age of six weeks, my husband and the doctor's assistant held down my child's legs and arms while the doctor performed the operation. My son was very strong, healthy and large for his age, and he fought so violently during the operation that the doctor remarked that he had had a frightful time with the baby, because he was already strong enough to fight back. I had stood on the porch of our home for three-quarters of an hour, listening to my baby's screams of agony while he was being circumcised. I suffered torments, listening helplessly to him, unable to ease his pain. After the operation, I went to him and the appealing and pitiful look on his little face tore my heart almost out of my body. I can still see his unhappy face. I hugged him to me and I cried because I was hurt as badly as my poor baby, and as I comforted him and dried his tears ever so tenderly, he fell asleep from exhaustion. The doctor said to me, 'Don't look so distressed. It didn't hurt him!' And this I denied, and said, 'Well, these are not tears of joy I am wiping away. It certainly did hurt him!' For three days, my baby suffered and his eyes were swollen from constant crying, because of the pain he endured."

But to continue with the description:

"Peri'ah: After the excision has ben completed, the mohel seizes the inner lining of the prepuce, which still covers the glans, with the thumb-nail and index-finger of each hand, and tears it so that he can roll it fully back over the glans and expose the latter completely. The mohel usually has his thumb-nail suitably trimmed for the purpose. In exceptional cases the inner lining of the prepuce is more or *less extensively adherent to the glans, which interferes somewhat with the ready removal;* but *persistent effort* will overcome the difficulty."

Yes, persistent effort will overcome the difficulty of tearing the skin which adheres to the prepuce.

I do not doubt for a moment that the strength of a man trained for this purpose, whose heart is as callous as stone, has the strength to do that very thing, despite the fact that nature had purposely adhered the prepuce to the skin for the purpose of *protecting* the organ until it is ready for the function for which it was intended to be used.

"Mezizah: By this is meant the sucking of the blood from the wound. The mohel takes some wine in his mouth and applies his lips to the part involved in the operation, and exerts suction, after which he expels the mixture of wine and blood into a receptacle (see Fig. 4) provided for the purpose. This procedure is repeated several times, and completes the operation, except as to the control of the bleeding and the dressing of the wound."

It is known and acknowledged as a fact that this

part of the procedure has caused the spread of various diseases. In fact, so serious did this become that in certain countries the sucking of the blood from the glans had to be abolished!

Doctor Mark Seth Reuben of New York reports in *The Archives of Pediatrics,* a case of tuberculosis following a ritual circumcision. He further states that "a review of the literature shows that there are reported 42 cases of tuberculosis infection following ritual circumcision," and warns that a mohel could infect many children "because the tubercle bacillus is found fairly constant in the mouths of tuberculosis patients."

Doctor Reuben states that an investigation revealed that in two cases, "the mohel presented evidence, clinical or bacteriological, of tuberculous infection." Also, that "tubercle bacilli were found in the sputa of four operators (mohelim)." Doctor Reuben further states that "systemic infection rarely occurs before the fourth month after circumcision. Without a single exception, every case, whether it recovered or died, showed tuberculous involvement of other tissues, glands or organs" and "of the 42 cases reported, 11 recovered, 16 died, and of the 15 (remaining) the final outcome is not known. Death usually takes place at about one year of age. . . ."

And yet "educated" people continue to talk about circumcision as being a health and hygienic measure.

"The remedies employed for the former purpose (bleeding) vary greatly among different operators and in different countries. Astringent powders enter largely into these applications. In North Germany the following mixture is extensively used: Dilute sulfuric acid, one part; alcohol, three parts; honey, two parts; and vinegar, six parts. A favorite remedy with many operators is the tincture of the chlorid of iron, which is a recognized efficient styptic. These solutions are applied by means of small circular pieces of linen with openings in the center, into which the glans is placed, and the dressing is closely applied to the parts below. This is secured in its place by a few turns of a small bandage. A diaper is now applied, and the operation is finished. The dressings are usually allowed to remain until the third day. The nurse in the meantime is instructed to apply olive-oil, plain or carbolized. When the parts are then uncovered the wound will in most cases have healed."

What about those children whose wounds do not heal?

"To guard against any mishap through *suppuration* or *erysipelas,* the genitals should be washed with soap and water, and afterward with a solution of bichlorid of mercury, 1 to 2,000. The mohel should deal similarly with his hands, and especially with his nails, using a nail-brush; and all the instruments to be used should be immersed in boiling water for about five minutes. The dressings should consist of sterile or antiseptic gauze or similar materials. All the preparations relating to the dressings, the instruments, and the hands of the operator should be made before the child is brought into the room in which the operation is to be performed, in order to avoid *unnecessarily prolonging the anxiety of the mother.* A basin with the bichlorid of mercury solution should be at hand, into which the operator may dip his hands imimmediately before he begins his work.

"Care must be exercised in *grasping* and making *traction* on the foreskin just before the knife is used. The outer layer is much more elastic than the inner; and if the outer and inner layers are not held firmly together at the margin, it may happen in making traction that the outer layer may become folded upon itself, with the result that the cut will remove a *circular piece of skin* just behind the edge of the foreskin. Of course this will require the *subsequent removal* of the *remaining edge.*

"Some operators dispense with the shield, but this is not to be commended; for it will expose the child to the risk *of having a piece of the glans cut off, and to dangerous bleeding in consequence."*

The above description of the operation contains a statement which, if made under ordinary circumstances and not associated with religious fanaticism, would be the cause of physical violence or to a suit at law for damages for a very substantial sum of money.

The mere mention that extreme care is necessary to prevent injury to the glans itself is proof that it has often happened in the past; otherwise, there would be no need for this reminder to be cautious, nor a warning to be careful not to "expose the child to the risk of having a piece of the glans cut off. . . ."

How many unfortunate children have been completely mutilated by this devilish operation, no one will ever know.

How can an operation be called "simple" when such extreme care must be exercised lest, in performing it, a worse mutilation takes place than the malady it was intended to correct?

"When the *operator uses his nails to tear the inner*

layer (peri'ah), he should be careful to have them absolutely clean. Should they not have the requisite shape or firmness, or should he prefer avoiding *any risk* attaching to that method, two pairs of short forceps may with advantage be substituted, and are now often used. The tear should be made carefully, so that it will not deviate greatly from the median line, and should not be *carried back too far;* for at the margin of the corona it might give rise to *unnecessary bleeding.* When the inner lining is tough, or bound down by adhesions, a *probe-pointed scissors may be used for the peri'ah.* Drs. Kehlberg and Lowe recommend the use of the scissors in all cases; claiming that the wound made by them is more favorable, and *infection less liable.* Against this, however, is the well-established principle in surgery that a *lacerated wound is less apt to bleed than one made by a sharp instrument."*

Note the instruction to the "operator" that in using his nails to lacerate the child's organ, he should be careful to have them absolutely clean. And we are told that circumcision is performed for hygienic reasons!

Note, also, the words that a lacerated wound is less apt to bleed, so for that reason this method is recommended, though obviously a more painful method than if a sharp instrument were used.

That such horrible methods are still used and that the menace of the spread of infection is equally present today from dirty and unclean circumcisers as it was before the advent of modern medicine is pertinently revealed in a warning by Rabbi Charles J. Shoulson of the Congregation Shomray Hadath, of Elmira, New York.

Rabbi Shoulson states that "a number of hospitals al-

Mohel Performing Circumcision

ready in this country have established prohibitive regulations because of one or two distasteful experiences with dishonorable and careless Mohelim," for, incongruous as it may seem, Mohelim are permitted to perform this operation in nearly all hospitals.

What the distasteful experiences were which the Rabbi speaks of are not mentioned in detail. Can it be that the children were permanently mutilated, or that they were infected with disease, or that they were horribly maltreated by "dishonorable and careless Mohelim?"

The good Rabbi issued his warning against Mohelim who appear for the ceremony in shameful exhibitions of carelessness and shabbiness, not only to improve their common decency and hygiene but also to prevent the complete outlawing of circumcision as a direct result of the discredit brought upon it by these utterly irresponsible and unfit men. Rabbi Shoulson wants circumcision to continue to be performed as a ritual ceremony, and says that "perhaps too few are familiar with the increasing difficulties that beset this ceremony so basic to our faith and the dangers that threaten its survival along traditional lines."

And what are the dangers that threaten its survival along traditional lines?

The first of these, he said, was because a considerable number of Jewish women "seem to think that it is just as proper to have a physician perform this ritual as a Mohel."

Here we have another confession of the religious

importance of this ritual performance. The question of health and hygiene claimed to be associated with it is not even mentioned!

However, he does emphatically assert that "there is no possible excuse for jagged or dirty fingernails" and calls for "minimum (hygienic) requirements for the Mohelim in every phase of their work."

What prompted Rabbi Shoulson to take cognizance of the "frightful amount of chaos and irresponsibility where this ritual is concerned?" It was when he saw for the first time a child being manhandled by a Mohel!

How many children has he seen manhandled since this first experience? And how long will the general public, our health authorities and the medical profession tolerate this condition? [2]

But to conclude the description of the operation from the *Jewish Encyclopedia:*

"Considerable opposition has of late years been made against the mezizah on the ground that it is entirely in conflict with the aseptic treatment of wounds, which should be adhered to in all instances, but more especially in consequence of a case in Cracow in which it became known that syphilis was communicated to a large number of Jewish children through an infected condition of the mohel's mouth. The result has been that a number of mohels have discarded the mezizah altogether. The majority of Jews, however, remain averse to such an innovation, the more so because it is condemned by the

[2] As this book goes to press, I have been reliably informed that Mohelim are no longer permitted to perform circumcisions in the Jefferson Hospital, Philadelphia, Pa., and in the New York Hospital, New York City.

Orthodox rabbis. As a compromise, which has received satisfactory ecclesiastical authority, a method has been adopted which consists in the application of a glass cylinder that has a compressed mouthpiece, by means of which suction is accomplished. Before the cylinder is applied a small quantity of sterilized absorbent cotton is placed in the mouthpiece, which effectually protects both the child and the operator."

What a confession! Circumcision responsible for an epidemic of syphilis!

And today, as an excuse for its continued practice, it is claimed that circumcision is a preventive of that very disease!

What a mockery! What an indictment!

And the Orthodox insist upon continuing such a method as part of the ritual of circumcision!

O! Religion! What chemical doth thou possess that can so stultify the human mind?

"The inner layer, when it is folded back, after its laceration, meets with the outer retracted layer, and the application of the dressing will satisfactorily keep the edges in fair apposition. Drs. Kehlberg and Lowe, in an article in Glassberg's work, recommend the closing of the wound by stitches after the method practised in surgery and known as the continuous suture. There are two objections to this treatment of the wound. It prolongs the operation unnecessarily, and entails the annoyance of removing the sutures when the union of the wound has taken place.

"The sponge, which has almost invariably been made use of for cleansing the parts (which are more or less covered with blood), should be entirely discarded. It has

been found difficult to keep sponges surgically clean; and
pledgets of sterile gauze—fresh ones for every case—are
to be preferred."

When describing the operation of circumcision, continued today under the pretense that it has health
and hygienic values, it is an insult to an intelligent mind
to be continually cautioned that unless extreme care is
taken, hygienic conditions will be violated and the
health of the child impaired.

"It prolongs the operation unnecessarily . . . it is difficult to keep the sponges surgically clean. . . ."

What a travesty!

> *"The most important consideration after the comple-*
> *tion of the operation is to guard against hemorrhage.*
> When the wound is limited to the prepuce itself, hemor-
> rhage need not be dreaded; for the pressure of the
> simple dressing alone will be sufficient to control it effectu-
> ally. Many operators apply a little tincture of iron, to
> which there can be no serious objection; for it is the
> most reliable of the remedies usually applied for the ar-
> rest of hemorrhage. The mohel should remain with the
> child for at least an hour to be perfectly satisfied that
> no hemorrhage follows, and to stop it should it occur.
> If the bleeding does not proceed from an artery, the
> tincture of iron with somewhat firmer pressure of the
> bandage will usually prove satisfactory. Should the bleed-
> ing come in jets, a catch-artery forceps must be applied,
> which acts as a clamp; *and a surgeon should be sent for,*
> *as a ligature may be needed."*

How long will modern society permit unskilled
hands to commit acts so potential with tragic results?

As I stated in a previous chapter, circumcision becomes a medical problem only after it has been performed.

Does one need more evidence to substantiate this statement than that contained in the description itself as just recorded from the authoritative *Jewish Encyclopedia?*

> "There is one form of bleeding which has thus far not been mentioned, and which needs consideration. It is well known that there are individuals who bleed very profusely and very persistently upon the slightest provocation. The old rabbis must have known of this condition; for they taught that, *when a mother lost two children from circumcision, those that might be born afterward should not be subjected to the operation.*"

Suppose she has no more boys, what consolation has this mother for having sacrificed two sons upon the altar of this savage superstition?

> *"This abnormal tendency to bleeding is of hereditary character.* It is transmitted through the mother and *through the daughters of such a mother.* The son, who might be a bleeder himself, will not transmit it to his children. Should such a condition be met with in circumcision, the ordinary methods for the arrest of hemorrhage must not be relied upon. The actual cautery will have to be resorted to, or a short piece of a metal or hard flexible catheter must be inserted in the urethra and firm pressure applied by means of a bandage. The catheter has the advantages of not interfering with urination, and of offering a firm surface for the application of pressure. It goes without saying that mechanical provisions must be made to prevent the catheter from slipping either in or out."

So much for the operation which many people think
is no more serious than cutting a hangnail with a pair
of scissors.

Only one whose sensibilities have not been dulled by
religion can fail to realize the indescribable pain and
torture involved in such an operation.

No, Madam Roland, it is not so much the crimes
committed in the name of Liberty that should shock us,
it is the crimes committed in the name of Religion that
should make us hang our heads in shame, and, with
Shakespeare, cry

> "O judgment thou art fled to
> brutish beasts, And men have
> lost their reason."

Chapter XI

ADULT CIRCUMCISION

I AM CONSTRAINED to record here the experiences of two young Christian men who had fallen in love with girls of the Hebrew faith. To show the depth of their devotion and the sincerity of their conversion, each underwent a circumcision operation.

The torture and agony they endured were truly manifestations of their sincerity. But they told me that had they known what they would suffer for their faith, they would have employed other means of showing their devotion. One of them said he would "never be the same again," and another, a reporter for a prominent New York newspaper, said, "It almost ruined me."

Is it any wonder!

To give some idea of how an adult suffers from this "simple" operation, here is a description of what happened to one man. These are the doctor's own words, in describing the patient's condition:

"The operation was performed in a proper manner by a surgical friend, but this friend, unfortunately, was a great believer in antiseptic and wet dressings. A few days after the operation he called upon me to ask me to go and see the patient, as they were both in a pickle, the patient being exceedingly angry, being in constant misery, and the penis so denuded by the giving of the sutures, owing to the erection, that it looked to the patient as if he never could have a whole penis again, and the doctor saw no way out of the difficulty; the penis was, in reality, a dilapidated and sorrowful-looking appendage and anything else but a thing of beauty or pride; it was raw, angry-looking, and bleeding at every move; the first wink of sleep was followed by an attempt at erection that raised the patient as effectively as an Indian would in scalping him; so that taken together, the penis, anxious countenance, and the flexed position of the whole body to relieve the tension on the organ, the man looked about as battered, cast down and sorrowful as Don Quixote in the garret of the old Spanish inn, with his plastered ribs and demolished lantern-jaw." [1]

This same physician, apparently well aware of the seriousness of circumcising an adult male, makes this further statement:

"A number of cases are on record where, owing to the want of that artistic and mechanical knowledge without which no surgeon is perfect, the operator has drawn forward the skin too tight in circumcising, after which, owing to the natural elasticity of the skin, the integument (outer covering or envelope of the organ) has retracted, leaving the penis like a skinned eel or sausage. This accident is even likely to occur where the skin has not been tightly drawn, but where the subsequent erections have

[1] Remondino, *loc. cit.,* pp. 303 and 304.

torn through the sutures, and where the natural retraction of the skin has laid the organ bare for some distance. This condition, where the penis is skinned like an eel or a sausage, is aggravated by unavoidable erections." [2]

After recording the above instances, I cannot help but ask: Would you go through such torture and endure such agony "to fulfill the covenant of blood atonement" as provided by the Hebrew ritual, to become a convert to Judaism and a member of the Congregation of the Children of Israel?

[2] *Ibid.,* p. 303.

Chapter XII

THE ANATOMY, MECHANISM AND FUNCTION OF THE PREPUCE

I DO NOT THINK man was born with a prepuce only to have it cut off at birth. The prepuce not only protects the glans penis from injury, but it also performs an important function during the mechanics of coitus.

The prepuce not only acts as a guard to protect the head of the glans penis from contact with other substances, but at the same time it keeps the corona in the sensitive state warranted by the tenderness of its flesh—more tender than a baby's skin—so that it will more readily respond to stimuli when it comes in contact with the vagina for coitus.

Even if the prepuce were of a rudimentary nature, which of course it is not, it should not be removed except for some definite medical reason. No more so than the vermiform appendix or the os coccyx.

While the vermiform appendix and the os coccyx have apparently no practical value, the prepuce not only has a definite purpose and is of beneficial use, but it is also a vitally important and essential part of the human anatomy.

In addition to the important function of protection, the anatomy of the prepuce when retracted adds extra bulk to the penis, which massages the corrugated walls of the vagina during coitus, thereby stimulating the flow of the coital juices and producing pleasurable sexual sensation in the female as well as the male, thus better preparing both for the orgasmic climax in unison.

The importance of the prepuce in the sexual act cannot be too strongly stressed.

In a paper read before the Academy of Medicine of Baltimore, Maryland, Doctor A. B. Arnold condemns circumcision because it deprives the glans penis not only of protection but of other valuable uses in the performance of its functions, particularly in the diminished sensitivity of the glans because of its continual exposure and contact with external substances.[1]

Doctor Arnold argued that "it is not difficult to divine the purpose of the prepuce, holding that it is necessary to protect the tactile sensibility of the glans, due to the presence of the Pacinian bodies in the nerves, and that a better provision than the anatomy of the prepuce cannot be conceived for shielding the very vascular and sensitive structure of the glans from external sources of irritation and friction, that might rouse the sensibility of the organ, which, on physiological grounds, may cause early masturbation; further arguing that, the corona being undoubtedly the most excitable part of

[1] Remondino, *loc. cit.*, p. 223.

the glans, its denudation by circumcision leaves it more apt to be affected by chance titillations." [2]

As a matter of fact, medical investigations in the field of sexual disorders have discovered that the removal of the prepuce is a definite contributing cause of masturbation. By the removal of the prepuce, the head of the penis is exposed to outside contact and stimulation, causing erections in many cases, which is the first step toward masturbation in the adolescent.

Even Doctor Remondino, who believes that circumcision is responsible for the "miraculous" preservation of the Jews, a panacea for nearly all the ills of mankind, and a sure cure for a pain in the thigh, admits that to many surgeons "the idea of circumcision . . . is looked upon as an unwarrantable operation, a procedure not only barbarous, painful and dangerous, but one that directly interferes with the intentions of nature," and that "the prepuce enjoys the same right to live and exist as the nose, the eye, or a limb. . . ." [3]

The prepuce not only has the same right to exist as any other part of the body, but it also possesses a definite and essential function which makes its removal as stupid and as criminal as to remove any other part of the body. The removal of one's teeth, in order to avoid brushing them every day, would be just about as sensible. And then, too, you would have the additional satisfaction of saving yourself all future trouble with your teeth. You would be completely free from the pain and annoyance necessary to preserve them.

[2] *Ibid.,* p. 223.
[3] *Ibid.,* p. 217.

However, there are some people who consider their teeth more precious than pearls and would not, under any circumstances, part with a single one unless absolutely necessary.

Every male animal is born with a prepuce—and lucky for them there is no Savage, Jealous Animal Deity to demand its removal as a blood atonement!

Doctor Paolo Mantegazza, one of the world's greatest authorities in the field of sexual behavior, states, "that the prepuce is an organ of pleasure in the male is beyond doubt," and he is equally certain that it augments the pleasure in the embrace of the woman, and then he brands circumcision as a scourge in these blistering words: "One thing I know, among civilized people, circumcision is a shame and an infamy." [4]

To add emphasis to his conviction, Professor Mantegazza then laconically exclaims, "I shall shout and continue to shout at the Hebrews, until my last breath: cease mutilating yourselves . . . !" [5]

In further reference to the subject, Professor Mantegazza suggests that women may be the best judge in the matter of whether the existence of the prepuce contributes to female sexual enjoyment. [6]

Such a test, in my opinion, would not be feasible nor conclusive for the very obvious reason that too many

[4] *The Sexual Relations of Mankind,* p. 99.
[5] *Ibid.,* p. 99. Professor Mantegazza must now include many non-Hebrews in his exhortation.
[6] *Ibid.,* p. 99.

factors are involved in coitus as far as the woman is concerned.

First, and most important of course, is the element of affectionate attachment. A woman may prefer one particular man above all others, regardless of the physical qualities involved.

Another important consideration may be the technique of one in preference to another. The approach of one man to the act of coitus is sometimes so radically different from that of another man that this element alone subordinates all other details involved in the act, not only as to the absence of the prepuce but even to the size of the glans itself.

The promiscuous woman would surely not be suitable for such a test. Her experience with a variety of men has dulled her sensitivity in this respect, and the physical appearance of the man, as far as she is concerned, is generally the most important element involved in sexual relationship.

A satisfactory test to determine whether the existence of the prepuce makes any difference in female sexual enjoyment might be this: If twins whose features, from face to glans, were identical, except that one was minus the prepuce, were to have sexual relations with the same woman under the same circumstances. Such a test, however, is too improbable, and even if consummated, the results, in a matter of such delicacy, would be far from conclusive.

The man, however, is the one most vitally concerned

in this matter, and he himself is the best judge as to whether or not the prepuce "is an organ of pleasure."

Doctor Robert L. Dickerson, in his valuable book, *Human Sex Anatomy,* in reference to this matter, suggests an inquiry from the woman's point of view, but states: "To be good evidence, it must be shown that this is based not on artistry but on anatomy." [7]

Those who are in a position to know from personal experience, and who are honest and frank about it, confess regret at its loss.

Doctor G. S. Thompson writes in the *British Medical Journal,* this significant confession: "At one time, when I accepted what authorities and books told me, I was such a believer in the orthodox cult of circumcision that I performed the operation upon myself; but increasing experience has convinced me of the unsoundness of this operation. . . . I would strongly urge that this, amongst many other unnecessary and evil mutilations, be relegated to limbo." [8]

Doctor Atkinson, with his unusual insight and scientific analysis, in discussing the importance of the prepuce, states that "the terminal part of the organ (glans penis) is covered by a delicate membrane and is highly sensitive. The function of the foreskin is to preserve this sensitiveness. Circumcision does away with this protection, the covering membrane becomes coarsened from exposure, and sensation is impaired.

[7] P. 82.
[8] March 27, 1924, p. 437.

Worse still, the point of the maximum sexual sensation is on the inner surface of the prepuce close to the frenum, and this point is bound to be removed. That the intensity of sexual sensation is impaired by circumcision is vouched for by men who have undergone the operation in adult life. This is surely an aesthetic tragedy that requires some justification, even if what you've never had you never miss." [9]

Aside from the fact that what you never had you never miss, you must remember that in order to deprive yourself of this greater enjoyment with the organ with which Nature endowed you, you must also endure an excruciatingly painful operation, thereby adding insult to injury.

Is there in the catalogue of man's stupidity a more perverse act?

[9] *Loc cit.,* p. 179.

Chapter XIII

RELIGIOUS FANATICISM AND
SEXUAL MUTILATIONS

No study of circumcision as a mutilation would be complete unless some reference were made and some facts recorded showing that man throughout history has resorted to various forms of sexual mutilation under the spell of religious superstition and frenzy.

Why man has selected the sexual areas of the body for particular abuse, it is difficult to determine with accuracy. But whatever the motive which prompted him to indulge in these acts of violence against the body, the fact remains that he has been guilty of it with unbelievable vengeance.

The seats of pleasure of the human body have always been the targets for religious abuse.

The perverted premise that the more you suffer here the less you will suffer "hereafter" has been the underlying doctrine responsible for this outrageous conduct. Existence on earth was considered a sort of purgatory. If you were happy, it was considered a form of depravity.

Religious dogma has gone out of its way to find ways and means of inflicting tormenting and distressing acts upon the individual.

Not even our sense of taste has been immune from this form of punishment, and we have been forced to eat "bitter herbs" so as to further chastise the body under this delusive spell and superstition that pleasure is a sin.

Fast days and periods of abstinence from foods we like are only too prevalent even in our time.

That many of these abuses of the body have been discontinued or greatly modified is proof that some progress has been made in emancipating man from the ignorant and superstitious past, and is encouragement to continue unabated our efforts in this field of education.

How far removed are those who insist upon having their sons circumcised from the brutal and heartless people who, in the Middle Ages, searched for innocent boys to force upon them the frightful mutilation of castration (remember, this was before the discovery of anaesthesia!) in order to secure soprano voices for the church choir, since women were not permitted to pollute the holy offices of Religion?

This infamous crime prevailed, despite the fact that fatalities due to castration amounted at times to more than fifty percent! Nor did the cries of anguish of those who survived, contribute in the slighest degree to its discontinuance.

Prior to the reign of Pope Clement XIV (1769-1774), it is estimated that as many as four thousand boys in the neighborhood of Rome alone were castrated in order to supply eunuchs for the choir.

In Paris less than a hundred years ago, a young priest castrated himself with the blade of a pair of scissors, and nearly lost his life from the subsequent hemorrhage.[1]

The opera singer Velutti, when a child, was castrated by his parents. Both of his testicles were removed. It was the intention of his father, who had performed the operation, that he enter the papal Chapel at Rome.[2]

There seems to be little doubt that the religious systems which imposed chastity upon their priests resorted to castration at one time to make certain that the edict would be obeyed, as too many were guilty of violating it.

Some interpret certain passages in the New Testament [3] as having a direct reference to castration, and many have sought to prove their application by their own self-mutilation. These self-inflicted acts have taken many and varied forms.

This is further substantiated by the fact that the first sect of castrates was founded by a disciple of one of the foremost of the Christian fathers, Origen. The sect was called "Valerians," and the name was taken from that of the founder, Arabic Valerius.

It is believed that this sect was the spiritual fore-

[1] Remondino, *loc. cit.*, pp. 89 to 92.
[2] *Ibid.*, pp. 89, 92, 108.
[3] See *Matt.* 3, vs. 10, 12; 5, vs. 28, 30; 18, vs. 8, 9; *Mark* 9, vs. 43, 47; *Luke* 23, v. 29; *Colossians* 3, v. 5.

runner of the Skopts which flourished in Russia at the beginning of the eleventh century.

This sect spread rapidly during the reign of Catherine II (1762–1796) and part of the reign of Alexander I. The operation of castration was performed by destroying the testicles with a hot iron, and the process was referred to as *baptism by fire*.

Milder methods were adopted in later times and the operation was accomplished by cutting off the masculine glans with a knife; if a hemorrhage followed, it was stopped by fire.[4]

In Moscow in 1733, a sect was discovered which undoubtedly was either related to or inspired by the Skopts. They were in the habit of practicing flagellation as a mortification of the flesh, but at night their holy prayers and dances produced the opposite of what was intended, and as a result many of the women became pregnant at these ceremonies.

This is not unusual in certain religious sects where cruelty, lust and asceticism go hand in hand. It is recorded that in this sect, at one of its "holy" banquets, the breast of a young girl was carved, and, having been cut into pieces, was passed around and consumed by those present. On another occasion, a young boy was killed and they drank his blood.[5]

However, the real purpose of the creed of the Skopts was complete asceticism and often they would remove

---

[4] Mantegazza, *loc. cit.,* pp. 105, 106.
[5] *Ibid.*

SKOPTS PRACTICING MUTILATION

the entire male organ. This was accomplished by binding the testicles and penis together in a noose so
that both could be amputated by a single blow of the
hatchet.[6]

That many died horrible deaths was no deterrent.
Nothing in the catalogue of human misery can arouse
a religious fanatic from the spell of delusion he is
under. The torture he suffers is only an additional con-
firmation of his faith.

All of these outrageous assaults upon the human
body are predicated upon the belief that the original
sin of mankind was not in the eating of the fruit of the
tree of knowledge but in the carnal union of Adam and
Eve, because it was the more pleasurable.

In 1866, an investigation was made of 5000 Skopts,
comprising 3900 males and 1400 females. Of the males,
588 had everything amputated, 833 had only the testicles removed, and 62 had mutilations of various
sorts. Among the females, 99 were found with amputation of the breast and pudenda; 308 had their breasts
missing, 182 were minus nipples, 251 had only their
genitals mutilated, and 108 had mutilations of various
sorts.[7]

Another sect of religious fanatics, in an effort to
stifle the sexual urge, wore on their prepuces enormous
rings and other contrivances as a sign of their chastity.
This they did by making a hole through the prepuce,
by which they fastened the rings. What their desires

[6] *Ibid.*, p. 107.
[7] *Ibid.*, p. 111.

were we cannot tell, but with these appendages they were unable to copulate.

These men were considered "holy" in the eyes of the women of the sect and many considered it an act of devotion to kiss the symbols.

Among the Maoris, many would bind the prepuce, as they considered it highly improper for the glans to be uncovered.[8]

The Coptic monks of Gisgeh would castrate their young Negro slaves, believing that castration was sanctioned by Biblical authority. The castration was most cruelly perpetrated. After the amputation of the sexual organs had been completed, the wound would be cauterized with boiling water and the victim struck down upon the dry sand, many unconscious, as if they were so many pieces of hated flesh.[9]

An authoritative article in Hasting's *Encyclopedia of Religion and Ethics* states, "In the religion of antiquity and the practices of modern savagery there is complete evidence of the mutilation of the human body as a definite part of the ritual," and "the only question which needs close attention is the relationship between religious rite and savage practice."[10]

In the same category with man's stupidity in the mutilation of the human body belongs the practice among certain savage tribes of knocking out a boy's tooth at puberty; the binding of Chinese women's feet; the Zulu custom of strapping the skull at infancy to

[8] *Ibid.*, p. 97.
[9] *Ibid.*, p. 105.
[10] Vol. 9, p. 62.

give it an elongated shape; the saucer-like stretching of the woman's lower lip among the Ubangis, and many others too numerous to mention here.

In addition to the laceration of the flesh, the chastisement of the mind to avoid satisfying the natural functions of the body is also a "mutilation."

Asceticism, celibacy, chastity, monasticism, are all forms of "mutilation," regardless of the area of the body selected for punishment or the method employed to accomplish it.

Infibulation, the deflowering of young girls, the cutting off of the clitoris, female circumcision, and other forms of sexual mutilation were all justified upon religious grounds, and the deeper the superstition, the more brutal the acts and the more tenacious the practice.[11]

The religious maniacs who practice these mutilations upon the body differ only in degree and not in kind from those religious fanatics who practice circumcision.

One is only slightly removed, by a diminished fanaticism, from the other.

---

[11] For a further and more detailed study of these monstrous acts of abuse of the human body, see Lewis, *The Ten Commandments;* Westermarck, *Origin and Development of Moral Ideas;* Mantegazza, *The Sexual Relations of Mankind;* Leuba, *The Psychology of Religious Mysticism;* Briffault, *The Mothers;* Tylor, *Primitive Culture,* and others.

Chapter XIV

STOP, IN THE NAME OF HUMANITY, STOP!

IT IS the duty of society to protect us from the brutality of tribal law. In man's progress from his primitive state to modern civilization, the great civilizing force is the humanizing of our savage instincts and the restraining of our brutal actions.

That is why today there have come into existence societies for the prevention of cruelty not only to animals, but to even our own children. So flagrant have been these acts that it has been necessary to write upon our statute books laws providing severe penalties for the unnecessary infliction of brutal physical violence.

Representatives of the Society for the Prevention of Cruelty to Children are forever vigilant in their fight against parents who heartlessly beat and maltreat their offspring, many of whom are scarred for life.

Court records of these acts of violence would be unbelievable were they not substantiated by the testimony of witnesses of unimpeachable integrity.

And yet, in many instances the brutality and pain inflicted upon children—for which men and women

have been convicted, and some even sent to prison—
do not compare, in violence, with the callous brutality
and torture inflicted upon helpless infants during circumcision.

Because of the religious association of circumcision,
a helpless infant is made the victim of a brutal sacrifice by the religiously blind, the superstitiously cruel
and the morally sadistic. Yet, these heartless people,
by wearing the cloak of religion, not only protect themselves from molestation, but also from responsibility
for their dastardly deeds.

I want to emphatically and unequivocally state here
and now that were circumcision proposed today for
the first time, it would be met with determined opposition and its proposer would be looked upon as a lunatic
fit only for the insane asylum.

If it were proposed for the first time today as a religious rite, it would be summarily dismissed as superstitious savagery.

If it were not "an unthinking habit," as Doctor Atkinson calls it, parents would shrink in horror from
such a suggestion which they would consider utterly
cruel and outrageously barbarous.

Such a proposal, were it made today for the first
time, would be treated with the same contempt as
would a suggestion that a child's toes or fingers be cut
off.

If it were seriously contemplated, mothers would
clutch their children to their breasts to guard them
against such an unwarranted attack, and would vent the

anger and resentment of aroused motherhood upon those who would propose such a foul deed.

Hundreds of brutal acts which man brought up from his savage state, and which bore the stamp of religion, have fortunately gone out of existence, due to the enlightenment of the human mind.

This has been accomplished, however, only in the face of bitterest opposition.

The history of the human race is filled with the heroic deeds of men and women who have labored for the good of mankind by defying outmoded conventions and destroying antiquated customs.

The enlightened Jews of Germany deserve our deepest thanks for their efforts in 1843 to abolish the practice of circumcision.

The following statement from the authoritative *Jewish Encyclopedia* is not without its significance today. It states that "after having for centuries been practiced as a distinctly Jewish rite, circumcision appeared to many enlightened Jews of modern times to be no longer in keeping with the dictates of a religious truth intended for humanity at large." [1]

And an important step toward the abolition of the rite of circumcision was made when the venerable Isaac M. Wise, the father of modern Judaism in America, at a Rabbinical conference in Philadelphia in 1869, proposed the abolition of circumcision upon converts to Judaism on the ground that it is "a measure of extreme cruelty when performed upon adults." This

---

[1] *Jewish Encyclopedia*, Vol. 4, p. 96.

proposal was finally adopted by the Reform Rabbis of America at a New York conference in 1892.[2]

If it is "extreme cruelty" for an adult to suffer circumcision, how much more monstrous to inflict such torture upon a helpless infant!

Like Thomas Paine, I have "no veneration for old mistakes—no admiration for ancient lies," and so I condemn circumcision as a survival of one of the insanities of religion based upon the ignorance and superstition of primitive man.

Nothing more need be said than that which has already been recorded in the pages of this book to prove that circumcision is a brutal and savage rite, without value and without one redeeming feature to recommend it.

If the facts presented in this book are not sufficient to convince some readers that circumcision should be abolished, I can only say that there exist among us some hopeless people whose mentality is so paralyzed by the narcotic of religion that nothing can arouse it from its state of lethargy.

But to the others, to those who have some regard for mankind, who believe that innocent and helpless children should be defended and protected from the savage brutality and cruel mutilation of circumcision, then to them I cry, with all the power and strength that I possess, with all the vehemence at my command, and from the deepest recesses of my heart, to *Stop, in the name of Humanity, Stop!*

[2] *Ibid.,* Vol. 4, p. 96. Also *Jewish Ceremonial Institutions and Customs,* p. 139.

BIBLIOGRAPHY

Barbarity of Circumcision, The, by Dr. Herbert Snow, Haldeman-Julius, 1948.
Behind the Mask of Medicine, Miles Atkinson, M.D., Scribner's, N.Y., 1941.
Catholic Encyclopedia, The, Encyclopedia Press, N.Y., 1909, 15 Vols.
Ceremonies of Judaism, The, by Abraham Z. Idelsohn, National Federation of Temple Brotherhoods, Cincinnati, Ohio, 1930.
Circumcision, by Felix Bryk, American Ethnological Press, N.Y., 1934.
Circumcision, by Dr. M. Clifford, J. & A. Churchill, London, 1893.
Devils, Drugs and Doctors, by Howard W. Haggard, M.D., Harper & Bro., N.Y., 1929.
Facts About Child Health, Federal Security Agency, Washington, D.C., 1946.
Folklore in the Old Testament, by Sir James George Fraser, Macmillan, N.Y., 1927.
Genital Sense, The, by Jacobus, Charles Carrington, Paris.
Golden Bough, The, by Sir James George Fraser, Macmillan, N.Y., 1927, 12 Vols.
Human Sex Anatomy, by Robert Latou Dickerson, M.D., Williams and Wilkins Co., Baltimore, Md., 1933.
Idiot Man, by Prof. Charles Richet, Brentano, N.Y.
Jewish Ceremonial Institutions and Customs, by Wm. Rosenau, Block Pub. Co., N.Y., 1929.
Jewish Encyclopedia, The, Funk & Wagnalls Co., 1916, 12 Vols.
Jewish Magic and Superstition, by Joshua Trachtenberg, Behrmens Book House, N.Y., 1939.
Lame, The Halt and The Blind, The, by Howard W. Haggard, M.D., Harper & Bro., N.Y., 1932.
Laws and Customs of Israel, by Gerald Friedlander, Shapiro, Ballantine & Co., London, 1929.
Marriage Manual, The, Dr. Abraham Stone, Simon and Schuster, N.Y., 1935.
Mind and Body, by Dr. Flanders Dunbar, Random House, N.Y., 1947.
Mothers, The, by Robert Briffault, Macmillan, N.Y., 1927, 3 Vols.
Mystic Rose, The, by Crawley, 2 Vols., Boni and Liveright, N.Y., 1927.
Origin and Development of Moral Ideas, by Edward Westermarck, Macmillan, London, 1924.
Origin and History of Hebrew Law, by J. M. Powis Smith, Univ. of Chicago Press, 1931.
Primitive Mentality, by Lucien Levy-Bruhl, E. P. Dutton & Co., N.Y., 1928.

Primitive and the Supernatural, The, by Lucien Levy-Bruhl, E. P. Dutton & Co., N.Y., 1928.

Psychic Trauma of Operation in Children, by Dr. David M. Levy, *American Journal of Diseases in Children,* July, 1945.

Psychopathia Sexualis, Dr. R. V. Kraft-Ebing, Physicians and Surgeons Book Co., N.Y., 1932.

Religion in Primitive Society, by Wm. D. Wallin, F. S. Crofts & Co., N.Y., 1939.

Religion of the Semites, The, by Wm. Robinson Smith, A. M. G. Black, London, 1927.

Science of Human Reproduction, The, by H. M. Parshley, Eugenics Pub. Co., N.Y., 1939.

Sexual Life of Savages, The, Prof. Bronislaw Malinowski, Eugenics Pub. Co., 1942.

Sexual Relations of Mankind, The, by Prof. Paolo Mantegazza, Eugenics Pub. Co., N.Y., 1935.

Social Background of the Old Testament, The, Hebrew Union College Press, Cincinnati, Ohio, 1942.

"Soul" of the Primitive, The, by Lucien Levy-Bruhl, Macmillan, N.Y., 1928.

Standard Bible Dictionary, The, Funk and Wagnalls, N.Y., 1936.

Ten Commandments, The, by Joseph Lewis, Freethought Press Assn., N.Y., 1946.

INDEX

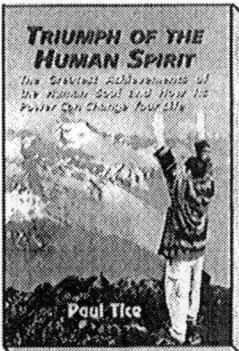

The Jumping Frog and 18 Other Stories: 19 Unforgettable Mark Twain Stories, by Mark Twain. This collection of Mark Twain stories has not been in print for many years and in this regard seems to be a new and rare collection. For example, out of the nineteen short stories contained here we found only two (*The Jumping Frog* and *Corn-Pone Opinions*) that were included in a larger collection commonly available called *Great Short Works of Mark Twain*. The Jumping Frog was the story that launched Mark Twain's career. He was loitering around the Angel's Camp mining town in California and was told the story in a worn out saloon by a bald-headed local who relayed the story to him in a dead-pan tone of voice, with no hint of excitement or humor. Twain wrote out the story and sent it to a humorist friend in New York, and it wound up being published in the prestigious *Saturday Press*. The story was copied and reprinted by newspapers throughout Europe and America, and Twain was on his way. These are great representative stories of Twain. They should make a good addition to libraries of collectors, or to classroom programs wishing to study the art of short story writing. More importantly, this rare volume should serve as a colorful and exciting addition to those who appreciate Twain's wit and wisdom. **ISBN 1-58509-200-2 • 128 pages • 6 x 9 • trade paper • $12.95**

Reason and Belief: The Impact of Scientific Discovery on Religious and Spiritual Faith, by Sir Oliver Lodge. Sir Oliver Lodge was a respected writer from the early twentieth century. At this time, there were a number of scientific advances that caused one to consider the ramifications of these new discoveries on the religious and spiritual beliefs of the day. But the impact of science may not be so great on spiritual matters in the final analysis, according to Lodge. He puts forth a number of interesting examples. He does not champion science as the final answer, which is what makes this book so interesting. Science is still helpful. It is a tool that is allowing us to reach spiritual answers that have so far not been found. Lodge actively searches for spiritual answers with great wisdom throughout the book and, when necessary, backs off from his great spiritual knowledge and explores our grasp of science to help us along. The last third of the book covers the scope of science. Lodge is a mystic who states that science is useful, but will never embrace the whole of knowledge. Thinking that science is and will be the final answer is the mistake in thinking that scientists of today fall into. They often ignore the seers and prophets of the past who have given us great spiritual truths. Scientists depend solely on a limited bandwidth of discipline that sometimes creates blinders, as found on a racehorse that can only run in a straight line. If the answer is off to the side, as part of the infinite world around us, it will never be seen. Lodge takes the blinders off, and opens us up to the larger possibilities around us. **ISBN 1-58509-226-6 • 180 pages • 6 x 9 • trade paper • $17.95**

Crux Ansata: An Indictment of the Roman Catholic Church, by H. G. Wells. When most people think of the great H. G. Wells what comes to mind are his science fiction books like *The War of the Worlds*, *The Invisible Man*, and others. Yet Wells was a brilliant man who was deeply interested in history and current events. He wrote this book at the height of World War II, just after he had resigned as Minister of Allied Propaganda. While in this position he became privy to information that totally shocked him concerning the Roman Catholic Church. Much of what he found is in this book. This book is clearly an indictment of the Roman Catholic church, as stated in the subtitle, not only based on what Wells had discovered during the war, but on his research of the Church throughout its entire existence. After this book was released a loud protest was issued from the Roman Catholic press accusing Wells, a respected writer and researcher, of spreading half-truths, innuendoes, and logical fallacies. Wells responded by saying that the church routinely engages in a complex, modern boycott of liberal thought that requires us to fight this intolerance with our own intolerance of the Roman Catholic system. This book has been swept under the rug of history, for the most part, because Wells was a famous person who openly and vocally questioned the status quo. Mark Twain is another good example—who wrote radical criticisms along religious lines, but publishers quietly sweep them aside and hope no one will look. **ISBN 1-58509-210-X • 160 pages • 6 x 9 • trade paper • $14.95**

Enuma Elish: The Seven Tablets of Creation, Volume One, by L. W. King. ISBN 1-58509-041-7 • 236 pages • 6 x 9 • trade paper • illustrated • $18.95

Enuma Elish: The Seven Tablets of Creation, Volume Two, by L. W. King. ISBN 1-58509-042-5 • 260 pages • 6 x 9 • trade paper • illustrated • $19.95

Enuma Elish, Volumes One and Two: The Seven Tablets of Creation, by L. W. King. Two volumes from above bound as one. ISBN 1-58509-043-3 • 496 pages • 6 x 9 • trade paper • illustrated • $38.90

The Archko Volume: Documents that Claim Proof to the Life, Death, and Resurrection of Christ, by Drs. McIntosh and Twyman. ISBN 1-58509-082-4 • 248 pages • 6 x 9 • trade paper • $20.95

The Lost Language of Symbolism: An Inquiry into the Origin of Certain Letters, Words, Names, Fairy-Tales, Folklore, and Mythologies, by Harold Bayley. ISBN 1-58509-070-0 • 384 pages • 6 x 9 • trade paper • $27.95

The Book of Jasher: A Suppressed Book that was Removed from the Bible, Referred to in Joshua and Second Samuel, translated by Albinus Alcuin (800 AD). ISBN 1-58509-081-6 • 304 pages • 6 x 9 • trade paper • $24.95

The Bible's Most Embarrassing Moments, with an Introduction by Paul Tice. ISBN 1-58509-025-5 • 172 pages • 5 x 8 • trade paper • $14.95

History of the Cross: The Pagan Origin and Idolatrous Adoption and Worship of the Image, by Henry Dana Ward. ISBN 1-58509-056-5 • 104 pages • 6 x 9 • trade paper • illustrated • $11.95

Was Jesus Influenced by Buddhism? A Comparative Study of the Lives and Thoughts of Gautama and Jesus, by Dwight Goddard. ISBN 1-58509-027-1 • 252 pages • 6 x 9 • trade paper • $19.95

History of the Christian Religion to the Year Two Hundred, by Charles B. Waite. ISBN 1-885395-15-9 • 556 pages. • 6 x 9 • hard cover • $25.00

Symbols, Sex, and the Stars, by Ernest Busenbark. ISBN 1-885395-19-1 • 396 pages • 5 1/2 x 8 1/2 • trade paper • $22.95

History of the First Council of Nice: A World's Christian Convention, A.D. 325, by Dean Dudley. ISBN 1-58509-023-9 • 132 pages • 5 1/2 x 8 1/2 • trade paper • $12.95

The World's Sixteen Crucified Saviors, by Kersey Graves. ISBN 1-58509-018-2 • 436 pages • 5 1/2 x 8 1/2 • trade paper • $29.95

Babylonian Influence on the Bible and Popular Beliefs: A Comparative Study of Genesis I.2, by A. Smythe Palmer. ISBN 1-58509-000-X • 124 pages • 6 x 9 • trade paper • $12.95

Biography of Satan: Exposing the Origins of the Devil, by Kersey Graves. ISBN 1-885395-11-6 • 168 pages • 5 1/2 x 8 1/2 • trade paper • $13.95

The Malleus Maleficarum: The Notorious Handbook Once Used to Condemn and Punish "Witches", by Heinrich Kramer and James Sprenger. ISBN 1-58509-098-0 • 332 pages • 6 x 9 • trade paper • $25.95

Crux Ansata: An Indictment of the Roman Catholic Church, by H. G. Wells. ISBN 1-58509-210-X • 160 pages • 6 x 9 • trade paper • $14.95

Emanuel Swedenborg: The Spiritual Columbus, by U.S.E. (William Spear). ISBN 1-58509-096-4 • 208 pages • 6 x 9 • trade paper • $17.95

Dragons and Dragon Lore, by Ernest Ingersoll. ISBN 1-58509-021-2 • 228 pages • 6 x 9 • trade paper • illustrated • $17.95

The Vision of God, by Nicholas of Cusa. ISBN 1-58509-004-2 • 160 pages • 5 x 8 • trade paper • $13.95

The Historical Jesus and the Mythical Christ: Separating Fact From Fiction, by Gerald Massey. ISBN 1-58509-073-5 • 244 pages • 6 x 9 • trade paper • $18.95

Gog and Magog: The Giants in Guildhall; Their Real and Legendary History, with an Account of Other Giants at Home and Abroad, by F.W. Fairholt. ISBN 1-58509-084-0 • 172 pages • 6 x 9 • trade paper • $16.95

The Origin and Evolution of Religion, by Albert Churchward. ISBN 1-58509-078-6 • 504 pages • 6 x 9 • trade paper • $39.95

The Origin of Biblical Traditions, by Albert T. Clay. ISBN 1-58509-065-4 • 220 pages • 5 1/2 x 8 1/2 • trade paper • $17.95

Aryan Sun Myths, by Sarah Elizabeth Titcomb, Introduction by Charles Morris. ISBN 1-58509-069-7 • 192 pages • 6 x 9 • trade paper • $15.95

The Social Record of Christianity, by Joseph McCabe. Includes *The Lies and Fallacies of the Encyclopedia Britannica,* ISBN 1-58509-215-0 • 204 pages • 6 x 9 • trade paper • $17.95

The History of the Christian Religion and Church During the First Three Centuries, by Dr. Augustus Neander. ISBN 1-58509-077-8 • 112 pages • 6 x 9 • trade paper • $12.95

Ancient Symbol Worship: Influence of the Phallic Idea in the Religions of Antiquity, by Hodder M. Westropp and C. Staniland Wake. ISBN 1-58509-048-4 • 120 pages • 6 x 9 • trade paper • illustrated • $12.95

The Gnosis: Or Ancient Wisdom in the Christian Scriptures, by William Kingsland. ISBN 1-58509-047-6 • 232 pages • 6 x 9 • trade paper • $18.95

The Evolution of the Idea of God: An Inquiry into the Origin of Religions, by Grant Allen. ISBN 1-58509-074-3 • 160 pages • 6 x 9 • trade paper • $14.95

www.ingramcontent.com/pod-product-compliance
Lightning Source LLC
Chambersburg PA
CBHW030017290326
41934CB00005B/381